Cambridgeshire
and the Fens

W A L K S

Compiled by
Brian Conduit

Fully revised by
Dennis and Jan Kelsall

Text: Brian Conduit
                        Revised text for 2008 edition,
                        Dennis and Jan Kelsall
Photography: Brian Conduit, Dennis Kelsall
Editorial: Ark Creative (UK) Ltd
Design: Ark Creative (UK) Ltd

Series Consultant: Brian Conduit

 This product includes mapping data licensed
from Ordnance Survey® with the permission
of the Controller of Her Majesty's Stationery
Office. © Crown Copyright 2010. All rights reserved. Licence number
150002047. Ordnance Survey, the OS symbol and Pathfinder are
registered trademarks and Explorer, Landranger and Outdoor
Leisure are trademarks of the Ordnance Survey, the national
mapping agency of Great Britain.

ISBN 978-0-7117-4980-1

While every care has been taken to ensure the accuracy of the route
directions, the publishers cannot accept responsibility for errors or
omissions, or for changes in details given. The countryside is not
static: hedges and fences can be removed, field boundaries can be
altered, footpaths can be rerouted and changes in ownership can
result in the closure or diversion of some concessionary paths. Also,
paths that are easy and pleasant for walking in fine conditions may
become slippery, muddy and difficult in wet weather, while
stepping stones across rivers and streams may become impassable.

If you find an inaccuracy in either the text or maps, please write
to Crimson Publishing at the address below.

First published 2002 by Jarrold Publishing
Revised and reprinted 2006, 2008, 2010.

This edition first published in Great Britain 2010 by Crimson
Publishing, a division of:
Crimson Business Ltd,
Westminster House, Kew Road, Richmond, Surrey, TW9 2ND
www.totalwalking.co.uk

Printed in Singapore. 4/10

A catalogue record for this book is available from the
British library.

Front cover: Punting on the River Cam
Previous page: Houghton Mill

Contents

The National Trust; The Ramblers' Association; Walkers and the Law; Countryside Access Charter; Global Positioning System (GPS); Walking Safety; Useful Organisations; Ordnance Survey Maps

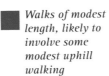

Short, easy walks

Walks of modest length, likely to involve some modest uphill walking

More challenging walks which may be longer and/or over more rugged terrain, often with some stiff climbs

Keymap

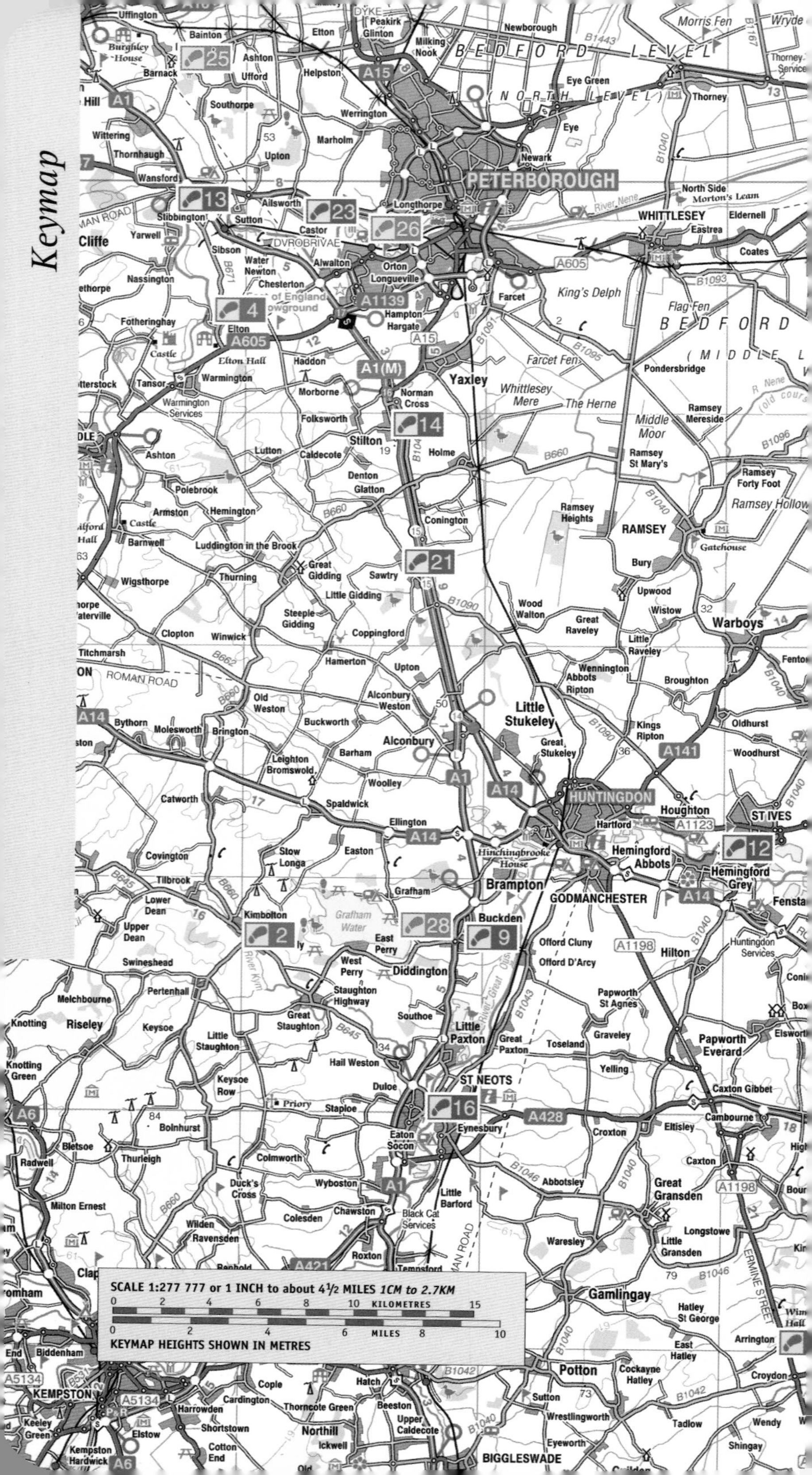

SCALE 1:277 777 or 1 INCH to about 4½ MILES 1CM to 2.7KM
0 2 4 6 8 10 KILOMETRES 15
0 2 4 6 MILES 8 10
KEYMAP HEIGHTS SHOWN IN METRES
PETERBOROUGH
BEDFORD LEVEL
(NORTH LEVEL)
BEDFORD
(MIDDLE LEVEL)
Uffington
Bainton
Burghley House
Barnack
Ashton
Ufford
Etton
Helpston
Peakirk
Glinton
Milking Nook
Newborough
Morris Fen
Wryde
Thorney
Eye Green
Eye
Newark
Southorpe
Wittering
Thornhaugh
Wansford
Upton
Marholm
Werrington
Stibbington
Sutton
Ailsworth
Castor
Longthorpe
DVROBRIVAE
Sibson
Water Newton
Alwalton
Orton Longueville
Chesterton
East of England Showground
Hampton Hargate
Farcet
King's Delph
Flag Fen
North Side
Morton's Leam
River Nene
WHITTLESEY
Eastrea
Eldernell
Coates
Cliffe
Yarwell
Nassington
Fotheringhay Castle
Elton
Elton Hall
Haddon
Warmington
Warmington Services
Tansor
Morborne
Norman Cross
Yaxley
Farcet Fen
Whittlesey Mere
The Herne
Pondersbridge
Middle Moor
Ramsey Mereside
Ramsey St Mary's
Folksworth
Stilton
Holme
Caldecote
Lutton
Ashton
Polebrook
Denton
Glatton
Conington
Armston
Hemington
Barnwell
Luddington in the Brook
Great Gidding
Sawtry
Little Gidding
Thurning
Wigsthorpe
Ramsey Heights
RAMSEY
Ramsey Forty Foot
Ramsey Hollow
Gatehouse
Bury
Upwood
Wistow
Warboys
Wood Walton
Great Raveley
Little Raveley
Steeple Gidding
Coppingford
Clopton
Winwick
Titchmarsh
ROMAN ROAD
Hamerton
Upton
Old Weston
Alconbury Weston
Wennington
Abbots Ripton
Broughton
Bythorn
Molesworth
Brington
Buckworth
Alconbury
Little Stukeley
Great Stukeley
Kings Ripton
Oldhurst
Woodhurst
Leighton Bromswold
Barham
Woolley
Catworth
Spaldwick
Ellington
HUNTINGDON
Hartford
Houghton
ST IVES
Covington
Stow Longa
Easton
Hinchingbrooke House
Hemingford Abbots
Hemingford Grey
Tilbrook
Lower Dean
Upper Dean
Kimbolton
Grafham
Grafham Water
Brampton
GODMANCHESTER
Buckden
East Perry
West Perry
Diddington
Offord Cluny
Offord D'Arcy
Hilton
Huntingdon Services
Swineshead
Pertenhall
Melchbourne
Knotting
Riseley
Keysoe
Staughton Highway
Great Staughton
Southoe
Little Staughton
Little Paxton
Great Paxton
Toseland
Papworth St Agnes
Graveley
Papworth Everard
Knotting Green
Hail Weston
Yelling
Keysoe Row
Duloe
ST NEOTS
Caxton Gibbet
Priory
Staploe
Eynesbury
Croxton
Eltisley
Cambourne
Bolnhurst
Bletsoe
Thurleigh
Radwell
Colmworth
Eaton Socon
Caxton
Duck's Cross
Wyboston
Abbotsley
Great Gransden
Milton Ernest
Colesden
Chawston
Black Cat Services
Little Barford
Wilden
Ravensden
Roxton
Waresley
Longstowe
Little Gransden
Gamlingay
Hatley St George
Arrington
East Hatley
Croydon
Biddenham
KEMPSTON
Cople
Hatch
Potton
Cockayne Hatley
Cardington
Harrowden
Thorncote Green
Beeston
Sutton
Wrestlingworth
Tadlow
Wendy
Shortstown
Elstow
Northill
Upper Caldecote
Eyeworth
Shingay
Keeley Green
Kempston Hardwick
Cotton End
Ickwell
BIGGLESWADE
ERMINE STREET
A1
A15
A1139
A605
A1(M)
A14
A141
A1123
A1198
A428
A421
A6
A5134
B1443
B1040
B1093
B1091
B1095
B660
B1096
B104
B1090
B662
B645
B1043
B1046
B1042
B671
25
13
23
26
4
14
21
2
28
9
16
12

St Mary • Tholomas Drove • Emneth Hungate • Stowbridge • A10 • Stow Bardolph • Wallington Hall • Stradsett

Guyhirn Gull • Begdale • Elm • Holly End • Wimbotsham • DOWNHAM MARKET • A1122 • Crimplesham

Guyhirn • A47 • Friday Bridge • Outwell • Stow Bardolph Fen • Barroway Drove • Bexwell • A134

Ring's End • Coldham • Upwell • A1122 • Denver • West Dereham

A141 • Laddus Fens • Three Holes • Popham's Eau • Nordelph • Fordham • Hilgay • River Wissey

Westry • Euximoor Fen • FEN CAUSEWAY • South District • Upwell Fen • Ten Mile Bank • Sugar Factory • B1160

MARCH • A1101 • Christchurch • Lakes End • Hilgay Fen • Southery • Methwold Fens

Town End • Binnimoor Fen • Tipps End • Welney • Wildfowl and Wetland Visitor Centre • Southery Fens • Methwold Fens

Manson Moor • Wimblington • 20 • Doddington • Wimblington Fen • Black Horse Drove • Brandon Creek • Little Ouse • Brandon Bank • Feltwell Anchor

Horseley Fen • Purls Bridge • Fodder Fen • Mare Fen • Apes Hall • Burnt Fen • Little Ouse River

CHATTERIS • A142 • Horseway • Welches Dam • Pymoor • Littleport • A1101 • Shippea Hill Sta

Chatteris Fen • Langwood Fen • Wardy Hill • Little Downham • West Fen • BEDFORD LEVEL • Chettisham • SOUTH LEVEL (S.L.)

1 • Mepal • Witcham • Coveney • 19 • 27 • Queen Adelaide • Prickwillow • A1101 • Kenny

Sutton • A142 • Wentworth • Witchford • Middle Fen • Stuntney • Great Fen • Mildenhall Fen

Hill Row Doles • Haddenham • Wilburton • Little Thetford • Stretham • Broad Hill • Isleham Fen • Thistley Green

North Hill • Aldreth • Stretham Services • Barway • Padney • Soham • Priory • Isleham Marina • Isleham

Willingham • Smithey Fen • Chittering • Upware • Wicken • Soham Mere • 17 • Frecker

18 • Fort • Rampton • North Fen • 11 • A1123 • Fordham • Chippenham

Longstanton • Cottenham • Denny Abbey • River Bank • Adventurers' Fen • Little Fen • Fordham Abbey • Landwade • Snailwell

Oakington • Westwick • Landbeach • Waterbeach • Reach • Burwell • B1103 • Exning • Moulton

5 • Histon • Impington • Clayhithe • Commercial End • 7 • Newmarket Services • A14 • NEWMARKET

Girton • A14 • Milton • Horningsea • Anglesey Abbey • 10 • Lode • Swaffham Prior • Newmarket Heath • A1304 • Cheveley

Ingley • A428 • Chesterton • Fen Ditton • Stow cum Quy • Swaffham Bulbeck • Bottisham • National Stud • Woodditon • Ditton Green • Kirtling

Coton • 8 • A1303 • Teversham • Little Wilbraham • A14 • Stetchworth • Burrough Green • Kirtling Green

CAMBRIDGE • A1134 • Cambridge Airport • Cherry Hinton • Great Wilbraham • A11 • Dullingham • Carlton

Comberton • Grantchester • Fulbourn • Six Mile Bottom • Westley Waterless • Brinkley • Weston Colville • Great Bradley

M11 • Trumpington • Gog Magog • 24 • Lark Hall • West Wratling • Weston Green • Little Bradley

Haslingfield • A10 • Great Shelford • Stapleford • Babraham • Balsham • Carlton Green • Great Thurlow • Little Thurlow

Harlton • Hauxton • Harston • Little Shelford • River Granta • A1307 • Little Abington • Great Abington

Barton • Newton • Foxton • Sawston • Whittlesford • Pampisford • Hildersham • Linton • 22 • A1307 • West Wickham • Withersfield • Great Wratling

Thriplow • Chapel • Duxford • Great Abington • 6 • Hanchett Village • HAVERHILL

Fowlmere • Hinton • Ickleton • Stump Cross • Hadstock • Bartlow • Shudy Camps • A1017 • A143

At-a-glance...

Walk	Page	Start	Nat. Grid Reference	Distance	Time
Barnack, Helpston and Ufford	76	Barnack	TL 078050	7½ miles (12.1km)	4 hrs
Buckden and Offord Cluny	30	Buckden	TL 191676	5½ miles (8.9km)	2½ hrs
Castor Hanglands	70	Castor	TL 123984	7 miles (11.3km)	3½ hrs
Elton	18	Elton	TL 089935	4¼ miles (6.8km)	2 hrs
Ely and Little Downham	83	Ely, Tourist Information Centre	TL 537802	10½ miles (16.9km)	5½ hrs
Ely and Little Thetford	58	Ely, Tourist Information Centre	TL 537802	7 miles (11.3km)	3½ hrs
Ferry Meadows, River Nene and Peterborough	80	Ferry Meadows Country Park	TL 148974	10¼ miles (16.5km)	5¼ hrs
Gog Magog Hills and the Granta Valley	73	Wandlebury Country Park	TL 492532	7 miles (11.3km)	3½ hrs
Grafham Water	87	Grafham Water Visitor Centre	TL 166680	9¼ miles (14.9km)	5 hrs
Grantchester Meadows and Cambridge	27	Grantchester	TL 433554	6 miles (9.7km)	3 hrs
Horseheath and West Wickham	22	Horseheath	TL 611472	4½ miles (7.2km)	2 hrs
Isleham	53	Isleham	TL 642743	7 miles (11.3km)	3½ hrs
Kimbolton	14	Kimbolton	TL 099677	3½ miles (5.6km)	1½ hrs
Linton, Hildersham and the Roman Road	67	Linton	TL 560468	7 miles (11.3km)	3¾ hrs
Lolworth, Knapwell and Boxworth	47	Lolworth	TL 366640	6 miles (9.7km)	3 hrs
Mepal and the Hundred Foot Drain	12	Mepal	TL 439813	3 miles (4.8km)	1½ hrs
Over and Swavesey	16	Over	TL 372707	4¾ miles (7.6km)	2½ hrs
Reach, Swaffham Prior and the Devil's Dyke	24	Reach	TL 567661	4½ miles (7.2km)	2½ hrs
Sawtry and the Giddings	64	Sawtry, St Judith's Lane car park	TL 170828	7¼ miles (11.7km)	4 hrs
St Ives, Houghton and the Hemingfords	38	St Ives	TL 314712	6 miles (9.7km)	3 hrs
St Neots and Little Paxton	50	St Neots, Riverside Park	TL 179601	7½ miles (12.1km)	4 hrs
Stilton and Folksworth	44	Stilton	TL 162893	6 miles (9.7km)	3 hrs
Stow cum Quy Fen	33	Lode	TL 533627	5½ miles (8.9km)	2½ hrs
Wansford, Sutton, Upton and Thornhaugh	41	Wansford	TL 075990	8 miles (12.9km)	4½ hrs
Wicken Fen	36	Wicken Fen, Nat. Trust car park	TL 564705	6 miles (9.7km)	3 hrs
Willingham and the Great Ouse	56	Willingham	TL 404704	6 miles (9.7km)	3 hrs
Wimblington and Stonea Camp	61	Wimblington	TL 415920	7¾ miles (12.5km)	4 hrs
Wimpole Park	20	Wimpole Hall	TL 338509	5 miles (8km)	2½ hrs

Comments

Three delightful limestone villages, all with fine medieval churches, are linked by tracks and field and woodland paths.

Buckden has a fine church and the remains of a bishops' palace, and there are extensive views across the valley of the Great Ouse on the walk to Offord Cluny.

The walk takes you through the lovely woodlands and across the open heathland of Castor Hanglands to the north of the River Nene.

This is an easy walk in the pleasant countryside of the Nene Valley, with the chance to visit a late-medieval manor house.

The towers of Ely Cathedral are seen from many different angles on this splendid and lengthy walk, mainly along drove roads, across the Isle of Ely.

The outward stretch is mainly across fields, the return leg is beside the Great Ouse, with almost constant views of Ely Cathedral.

The route combines a circuit of Ferry Meadow Country Park with a walk along the banks of the River Nene. The longer walk includes the centre of Peterborough and the cathedral.

From an Iron Age fort on the Gog Magog Hills, the route descends into the Granta Valley. A walk through the valley is followed by an easy climb onto a ridge for a superb climax along a tree-lined Roman road.

This extended circuit of the reservoir includes two villages, varied walking and fine views across the water.

A popular walk with residents, this is a great way to reach the heart of Cambridge and explore its wealth of fascinating buildings.

Rambling the gentle hills of eastern Cambridgeshire, this walk links two quiet villages and gives some fine views over the surrounding countryside.

This flat Fenland walk to the south and west of Isleham uses tracks, field paths and part of a disused railway line.

The walk takes you onto the low hills to the north of Kimbolton and there are fine views over the village on the descent.

After climbing a ridge, the route continues along a stretch of Roman road before descending into Hildersham and through the Granta Valley.

This walk, mainly along broad tracks, is in the gently undulating countryside to the south of the Great Ouse and links three quiet villages.

The first and last parts of this short and easy walk are beside the Hundred Foot Drain, dug as part of the 17th-century drainage of the Fens.

Two Fenland villages in the valley of the Great Ouse are linked by tracks, field paths and embankments. There are wide views across the Fens.

This route includes two attractive Fenland villages and ends with a walk along the Devil's Dyke, a Dark Age defence and fine viewpoint.

The walk is across gently undulating country to the south-west of Peterborough, visiting two small hamlets, one of which has great historical interest.

A perfect riverside walk, which starts in a historic town and includes three picturesque villages, medieval churches, thatched cottage, old mill and beautiful meadows.

A relaxing walk from the town through old meadows by the River Great Ouse to a nearby nature reserve that has been created from abandoned sand and gravel workings.

From the village of Stilton, the route takes you across undulating country, passing the site of a deserted village and the earthworks of a motte-and-bailey castle.

An attractive walk across open fenland is enhanced by a pretty village, old mill, tree-lined channel and the chance to visit a restored 17th-century house.

This route to the west of Peterborough takes in four attractive villages and includes some splendid walking beside the River Nene.

This walk takes you around the edge of the National Trust's Wicken Fen Nature Reserve, one of the few remaining areas of undrained fenland.

Wide and straight tracks link Willingham with the Great Ouse, and the middle stretch of the walk is along an embankment above the river.

This Fenland walk of wide and extensive views take you from the village of Wimblington to the earth-works of a Roman fort.

A large and imposing country house and fine views across the extensive parkland are the chief attractions of this walk.

Introduction to Cambridgeshire and the Fens

Statistically, Cambridgeshire is the flattest county in England. Although its highest point – at Great Chishill in the south of the county, near the Hertfordshire and Essex borders – rises to 480ft (146m), this is exceptional, and the average height is considerably lower. On an Ordnance Survey map of the Fens, contour lines are virtually non-existent. The Fens cover a considerable part of Cambridgeshire and feature prominently in this walking guide, but there is more to the county than their flat expanses. Gently undulating country and some hills, albeit fairly low ones, are to be found in the west and south.

Riverside scenery and historic landscapes

Despite what enthusiastic hill-walkers often say, flat terrain is neither boring nor featureless, and Cambridgeshire has much to offer walkers. This includes some lovely riverside scenery, fine old towns, attractive villages and much of historic interest, all set within a pleasant and gentle landscape. The Fens themselves are of great interest to those keen on landscape history and development, and their immense flatness does have a uniquely fascinating quality that is difficult to define, perhaps possessing something of the attraction of the desert wastes of the Sahara or the polar wastes of the Arctic. Much of the walking in the Fens is along straight, broad drove roads or on the top of embankments above the rivers and drainage channels, from which you can fully enjoy the wide and expansive views.

Attractive villages

Cambridgeshire was one of the counties that was enlarged as a result of the boundary changes of 1974. The north-west used to be in Northamptonshire – the historic Soke of Peterborough. This is limestone country, part of the belt of oolitic limestone that runs in a north-easterly direction from the Cotswolds to Yorkshire. This gently undulating landscape, watered by the beautiful River Nene, contains villages which, though less commercialised, are just as attractive as many of their better-known Cotswold counterparts.

Fine old market towns, water and chalk hills

The west is the former small county of Huntingdonshire, also absorbed into Cambridgeshire in 1974. This contains a slice of Fenland but also much undulating country. The area is noted for the string of fine old market towns and picturesque villages located near the banks of the Great Ouse. A more recent feature of the landscape is Grafham Water, a large reservoir created in the 1960s. It has now become an important wildlife and recreational area, particularly valuable in a county lacking in natural lakes. Almost as valuable an asset are the cluster of lakes in the valley of the Great Ouse around St Ives, Huntingdon and St Neots, created from the extraction of sand and gravel.

Barge on the River Nene

The hilliest country in Cambridgeshire is to be found in the south, near the Essex and Hertfordshire borders. Here there is a series of chalk outcrops, forming part of the chalk range which extends across eastern England from the Chilterns. One of these outcrops is the Gog Magog Hills, topped by the Iron Age hillfort of Wandlebury Ring, now the focal point of a popular country park within easy reach of Cambridge.

The Fens

The Fens are undoubtedly the dominant feature of the Cambridgeshire landscape, extending over much of the central, eastern and northern parts of the county and spreading over the borders into neighbouring west Norfolk and south Lincolnshire. Centuries ago the whole area was a vast expanse of water and marsh, inhabited by people who lived on the drier 'islands' which rose above the waterlogged lowlands, eking out a living from fish, eels and wildfowl. It was on these marshlands – difficult to penetrate without knowledge of the terrain – that the semi-legendary Saxon hero Hereward the Wake held out against the Norman conquerors for many years after 1066.

From the earliest days man tried to use the Fens, and a process of gradual reclamation of the land for farming took place. In the Middle Ages this was spearheaded by the many great monasteries in the area but it was not until the 17th century that the drainage of the Fens began on a large and systematic scale. The men mainly responsible for initiating this were the fourth Duke of Bedford and the Dutch engineer Cornelius Vermuyden. Vermuyden's major project involved the digging of two parallel channels about 21 miles (34km) long between Earith and Denver – the Old and New Bedford rivers – leaving an area in between (the Ouse Washes) that could absorb flooding in the winter and be used as pasture in the summer. This and other schemes were bitterly opposed by local people because it

Introduction

threatened their traditional fishing and wildfowling rights, but the schemes
went ahead and by the 19th century most of the Fens had been drained and
converted into what is now an intensive and highly productive area of
vegetable, flower and fruit growing.

There are few places left where you can see some of the original
undrained Fenland but one is Wicken Fen, roughly halfway between
Cambridge and Ely. This is Britain's oldest nature reserve and is maintained
by the National Trust.

Cambridge and Grantchester

The Great Ouse is the county's principal river and Cambridge, one of
England's finest and most distinctive historic cities, is situated on the
banks of one of its tributaries, the Cam. The Norman conquerors built a
castle here in the late 11th century, the first scholars arrived in 1209 and
the first college (Peterhouse) was founded in 1284. It is the combination of
river and college buildings that gives Cambridge its unique charm. As the
Cam meanders along the 'backs' of the colleges, it makes a delightful scene,
flowing between willow-lined banks, under a variety of bridges, with
people punting or rowing, especially on languid summer afternoons. Finest
view of all from the river is probably that of King's College Chapel, a
building of perfect proportions and quite breathtaking beauty.

A short distance upstream from Cambridge is the idyllic village of
Grantchester, easily reached by boat or across Grantchester Meadows by
bicycle or on foot. Rupert Brooke lived here before the outbreak of the First
World War and immortalised the village in his nostalgic poem *The Old
Vicarage, Grantchester.* After the war it became a major artistic and
intellectual centre, and something of the flavour and atmosphere of those
days can still be sampled by sitting under the trees in the garden of the
Orchard Tea Rooms, a traditional haunt of many visitors to Grantchester.

Ely, Peterborough, stately homes, Stonea and Devil's Dyke

Apart from the Cambridge colleges, the foremost historic attractions of
Cambridgeshire are the great Norman cathedrals of Ely and Peterborough.
In particular Ely, situated on one of the Fenland 'islands', ranks as one of
the outstanding cathedrals of Europe and appears almost to float above the
surrounding flat terrain. There are smaller monastic remains at Thorney,
Ramsey, Denny and Isleham, and the county's fine stately homes include
Wimpole Hall, Anglesey Abbey, Elton Hall and Hinchingbrooke House.
Wimpole Hall is probably the most imposing of these, set in lovely rolling
parkland near the Hertfordshire border.

Other historic attractions include the Roman fort at Stonea Camp near
March, the old bridge over the Great Ouse at St Ives, with its rare medieval
chapel – one of only four in England – and a number of outstanding parish
churches. Two historic features provide some superb walking: the Roman

Approaching Elton church

road that runs along the chalk ridge and the Devil's Dyke, an impressive Dark Age earthwork.

Walking in the area

There are a number of long-distance routes in Cambridgeshire – Fen Rivers Way, Nene Way, Ouse Valley Way, Icknield Way, Hereward Way and so on – which provide pleasant, easy-to-follow and satisfying walking, and most paths are well-waymarked.

Obviously in a walking guide to an area like this, there are no really difficult or challenging routes so the orange-coded walks are placed in that category purely because of their length. The greatest difficulties a walker is likely to encounter are muddy conditions after rain or during winter months and overgrown paths and tracks in the middle of summer, especially on those tracks tightly enclosed by trees and hedges. This is a small price to pay for the enjoyment of a combination of gently undulating slopes, wide and open expanses, huge skies, lazily winding rivers, appealing old towns and attractive villages, which are all ingredients of the Cambridgeshire landscape.

A final point is that, during the winter, some of the riverside meadows, especially those beside the Great Ouse, are regularly flooded. This is likely to affect parts of Walks 12, 16 and possibly others. If this occurs, you can complete the walks by using the adjacent roads.

With the introduction of **'gps enabled' walks,** you will see that this book now includes a list of waypoints alongside the description of the walk. We have included these so that you can enjoy the full benefits of gps should you wish to. Gps is an amazingly useful and entertaining navigational aid, and you do not need to be computer literate to enjoy it.

GPS waypoint co-ordinates add value to your walk. You will now have the extra advantage of introducing 'direction' into your walking which will enhance your leisure walking and make it safer. Use of a gps brings greater confidence and security and you will find you cover ground a lot faster should you need to.

For more detailed information on using your gps, a *Pathfinder Guide* introducing you to gps and digital mapping is now available. *GPS for Walkers*, written by experienced gps teacher and navigation trainer Clive Thomas, is available in bookshops (ISBN 978-0-7117-4445-5) or order online at www.totalwalking.co.uk

Mepal and the Hundred Foot Drain

		GPS waypoints
Start	Mepal, parking spaces where road ends on west side of Mepal Bridge	
Distance	3 miles (4.8km)	
Approximate time	1½ hours	
Parking	By Mepal Bridge	
Refreshments	Pub by Mepal Bridge	
Ordnance Survey maps	Landranger 143 (Ely & Wisbech), Explorer 228 (March & Ely)	

GPS waypoints

- 🖉 TL 439 813
- Ⓐ TL 445 817
- Ⓑ TL 449 806
- Ⓒ TL 439 805
- Ⓓ TL 434 805

Mepal is one of the small settlements dotted in the fens surrounding Ely and overlooks the two great channels that drain the Bedford Levels to the Wash. The walk encircles the village, taking in an interesting reserve that Nature has reclaimed from old clay diggings.

Unlike many of the small villages in the area, Mepal bears little obvious trace of its antiquity. Its older houses date mainly from the latter part of the 19th century, when a plainer, pragmatic style of brick superseded the traditional vernacular that sprang from timber frame. The reason is a devastating fire that occurred around the 1860s, which destroyed many of the original buildings.

The New Bedford River or Hundred

The Three Pickerels

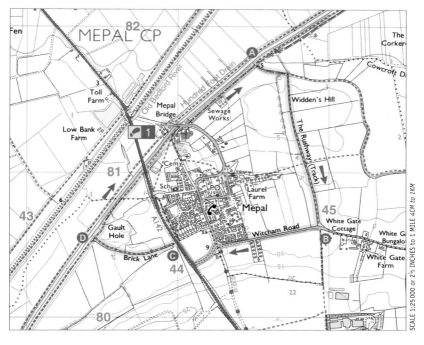

SCALE 1:25000 or 2½ INCHES to 1 MILE 4CM to 1KM

| 0 | 200 | 400 | 600 | 800 METRES | 1 |
| 0 | 200 | 400 | 600 YARDS | ½ |

KILOMETRES
MILES

Foot Drain (from its width) and its parallel channel to the north, the Old Bedford River were engineered by Cornelius Vermuyden in 1650 to drain the fen for improved agricultural use. They run dead straight for some 20 miles (32km) between Earith and Denver Sluice and the mile-wide tract of low-lying land between them serves as a great reservoir to absorb winter floods.

From the end of the lane, recross Mepal Bridge and turn through a gate on the left, from which a track runs beside the flood embankment containing the Hundred Foot Drain. After a generous ¼ mile (400m) the track dips to cross a brick bridge. Turn off immediately beyond in favour of another track beside the ditch **A**. Reaching a fork, some 250 yds (229m) along, bear right along The Rushway, a grass track dogging the field edge. Ahead, in the distance is the imposing tower of Sutton's church. Later becoming enclosed between tunnel-like hedges it leads to a lane **B**. Go right, and at the end left to reach the main road. Cross with care and follow the verge right for 200 yds (183m) to find a field access **C**. From it a hedged path, Brick Lane, leads to the old clay workings of Gault Hole. Through a kissing-gate at the end climb an embankment and follow it left past the reedy pool, mounting a stile at the end to reach the Hundred Foot Drain **D**.

Immediately drop right to a second stile concealed in the bushes below, from which a wooded path continues between the river and pool. Later passing flood meadows, the path leads to a bridge carrying the main road. If the path beneath the bridge is impassable because of flood, escape over the fence and cross the road, stepping over a stile beyond to regain the riverbank. The ongoing path ends beside the Three Pickerels, just off the lane at Mepal Bridge. ●

Kimbolton

			GPS waypoints
Start	Kimbolton		TL 099 677
Distance	3½ miles (5.6km)		Ⓐ TL 099 678
Approximate time	1½ hours		Ⓑ TL 102 679
Parking	Kimbolton, parking spaces in High Street		Ⓒ TL 112 692
			Ⓓ TL 116 688
Refreshments	Pubs and coffee shop at Kimbolton		Ⓔ TL 109 679
Ordnance Survey maps	Landranger 153 (Bedford & Huntingdon, St Neots & Biggleswade), Explorer 225 (Huntingdon & St Ives)		

The walk wanders the gentle slopes of Warren Hill, which rises to a height of 232ft (71m) to the north of Kimbolton. The views are fine and extensive, especially on the descent, where the town, church and imposing mansion of Kimbolton Castle are spread out below.

Kimbolton's spacious High Street is lined with fine buildings and has a soaring medieval church at one end and a sweeping Robert Adam gatehouse fronting the castle at the other. The ancient castle was acquired by the Montagus in 1615, who brought in Sir John Vanbrugh, the playwright cum architect who was also responsible for Castle Howard and Blenheim Palace to restyle it a century later. It remained the family seat until 1950 when it was sold to become Kimbolton School. In the church is a beautiful 14th-century rood screen with colourful panels depicting the saints, while carvings of a foliate Green Man and the Devil decorate the top rail. Nearby is a rare English example of a stained glass window by Louis Comfort Tiffany. It was commissioned by Consuelo, Dowager of the eighth Duke of Manchester as a memorial to her daughters. Disinclined to follow his father into the jewellery trade, Louis studied art and developed the coloured, opalescent decorative glass that made his art nouveau lampshades so distinctive. The window is doubly unusual in that it depicts a religious scene, for in America, Tiffany's more usual subject matter for his windows was landscape or abstract.

Tiffany stained glass window

From Castle Green, by the grand entrance to the school, walk up High Street and curve around the church. As the road then bends left, keep ahead into Carnaby **Ⓐ**. Its two branches combine to cross the River Kym in front of the cemetery gates. Skirt the cemetery to the left, meeting a narrow lane at the end. Turn left and immediately right, going right again along a track that runs behind cottages and then past allotments.

Reaching a junction just after them **Ⓑ**, turn left up a tall-hedged grass track. Later opening out on the right, it continues gently uphill to the edge of Warren Spinney. Slip through a gap in the hedge and carry on alongside the wood. Beyond its northern corner, keep going over the brow of the hill to join a concrete track. Follow it around a bend and immediately go right, in time arriving at another junction. The track to the right ultimately winds out to Bigram's Lane **Ⓒ**.

Turn right and walk to Bigram's Farm. On the right, just before a T-junction **Ⓓ**, a bridleway leads beside the farm into the corner of a large field. It undulates with the right-hand boundary for almost $^3/_4$ mile (1.2km), eventually passing Warren Spinney. At the far end of the trees, a broad gap in the accompanying hedge affords access into the adjacent field **Ⓔ**.

Strike a diagonal out from the corner along a clear path through the crop, enjoying a magnificent view across the village. Entering the next field, take a slightly sharper angle to its far corner, there recrossing the River Kym to emerge onto the main road. To the right it winds back into the centre of the village. ●

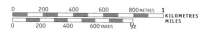

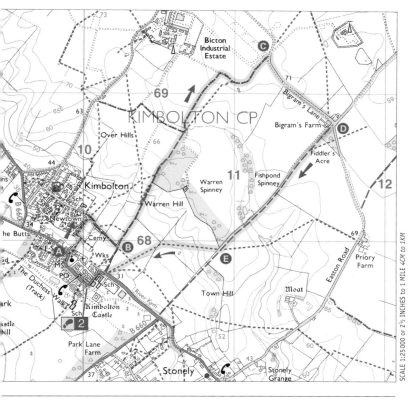

Over and Swavesey

Start	Over
Distance	4¾ miles (7.6km)
Approximate time	2½ hours
Parking	Small car park beside church
Refreshments	The White Horse Inn at Swavesey
Ordnance Survey maps	Landranger 154 (Cambridge & Newmarket), Explorer 225 (Huntingdon & St Ives)

GPS waypoints

- 🖉 TL 372 707
- Ⓐ TL 370 704
- Ⓑ TL 362 710
- Ⓒ TL 352 700
- Ⓓ TL 362 691
- Ⓔ TL 361 689
- Ⓕ TL 373 700

This undemanding walk straddles the Greenwich Meridian and follows Swavesey Drain to the River Great Ouse. After striking across fields to Swavesey, where there is a convenient pub, it returns past old orchards. The churches of both villages hold interest and there are pleasing views from the relative heights of the embankments that contain the watercourses.

Medieval Over was one of the largest settlements in the area and, like its neighbour Swavesey, was dependent for transport and communication on the Great Ouse. Locally grown woad was used to produce a blue dye, an industry that brought relative prosperity to the village. This wealth is reflected in the development of its church, originally Saxon, but rebuilt with stone brought across the marshes from Barnack, almost 30 miles (48km) away. An unusual feature is the stone bench around the walls, seating for the elderly at a time when the congregation was expected to stand or kneel throughout the service.

🖉 Leaving the small parking area, follow the lane past the church. After some ¼ mile (400m), turn off into Lowburyholme Road Ⓐ, signed as a footpath to Overcote. Degrading to a track, the way continues between outgrown hedges. Swing left in front of the entrance to a field and later cross a stile before climbing onto a flood embankment. To the right, a path follows the crest above Swavesey Drain, dug to take barges from the river to a wharf at Swavesey.

Reaching Webbs Hole Sluice Ⓑ, turn across the bridge and walk forward on another embankment that soon curves parallel with the river. Pleasure boats pass to and fro and, across the low-lying fields to the left, a tapering spire and square tower mark the churches of Over and Swavesey respectively. Follow the raised path, crossing occasional stiles for one mile (1.6km), eventually reaching a fork beside a bridged lock Ⓒ. Swing left in front of it and then, just before a stile, go left again, dropping to a meandering path beside Navigation Drain. At its end, turn right onto a track which crosses a disused railway line and soon leads to Ⓓ.

The church lies a short distance to the left, set back from the road behind its extensive graveyard. It stands on the site of an early priory, established before the Normans arrived on these shores. Inside, the ends of each pew are decorated with a carved head, some dating from the 15th century whilst others are Victorian copies of the originals.

The onward route, however, lies to the right, winding through the village to a junction beside the White Horse Inn 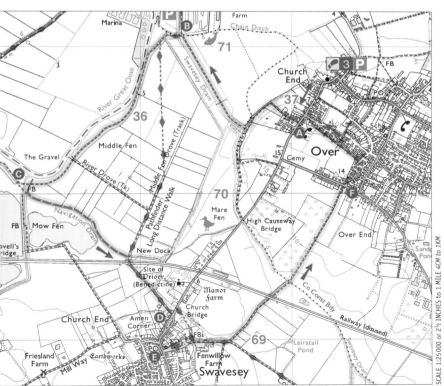. Turn beside it into Market Street, walking on the right-hand side to continue past the village green. Degrading to a track, the way subsequently forks and you should take the left branch signed to Over. Breaks in the hedge allow a view back to the church, in front of which is the part-timbered building of Manor Farm. Carry on, recrossing the old railway line and later a drain, where to the right, a windmill can be seen in the middle distance – one of many that once dotted the Fens. Keep on past a succession of fruit orchards, at the far side of which, a farm track leads out to a lane **F**.

Cross diagonally right to an enclosed

The White Horse Inn at Swavesey

footpath that winds into a small housing estate. Emerging onto a street, follow it ahead and then left. After passing Denny Close, turn off left along a pleasant tree-lined grass track that skirts the houses. Meeting another street at the far end, swing right back onto the estate and then go left, walking out to the main lane. Retrace your outward steps right back to the church.

Elton

		GPS waypoints
Start	All Saints' Church, Elton	TL 089 935
Distance	4¼ miles (6.8km)	**Ⓐ** TL 092 928
Approximate time	2 hours	**Ⓑ** TL 089 916
Parking	Roadside parking at Elton	**Ⓒ** TL 077 915
Refreshments	Pub at Elton and café at Elton Hall garden centre	**Ⓓ** TL 084 937
Ordnance Survey maps	Landranger 142 (Peterborough), Explorer 227 (Peterborough)	

This uncomplicated walk straddles the Cambridgeshire – Northamptonshire border, exploring the pleasant Nene Valley countryside south of the village of Elton. There are glimpses during the latter stage across the park to Elton Hall. Home of the Proby family since 1660, it is open to the public and stands amidst exquisite gardens.

Elton Hall (tel. 01832 280468) stands on the site of a Norman manor and was begun by Sir Peter Proby, Lord Mayor of London and Comptroller of the Royal Household after being granted the estate by Elizabeth I. The superb decorations, furnishings and art treasures reflect the changing styles during its 350 years as a family home, an evolution most recently expressed in the Gothic orangery and garden created to celebrate the millennium.

Beside Blue Bell Spinney

Head from the church along the B671, passing the Black Horse Inn and later the entrance to Elton Hall. Reaching the busy main road, carefully cross and go left to turn up a private lane onto the Elton Estate **Ⓐ**. Abandon it just a short distance along through a waymarked gate on the right and strike across the field to another gate by the corner of a wood. Keep ahead at the perimeter of the next field, joining a track at its far side that runs ahead beside Blue Bell Spinney.

Reaching the end of the wood, the track swings right and left along the field edge. A copse at the far side is side-stepped to the left before crossing a plank bridge through a gap in the hedge to gain the next field. Keep with the right-hand boundary to resume your southerly heading, soon arriving at a T-junction **Ⓑ**.

To the right, the track runs between open fields for over ½ mile (800m), eventually ending at a lane. Go left, shortly bending with it in front of a

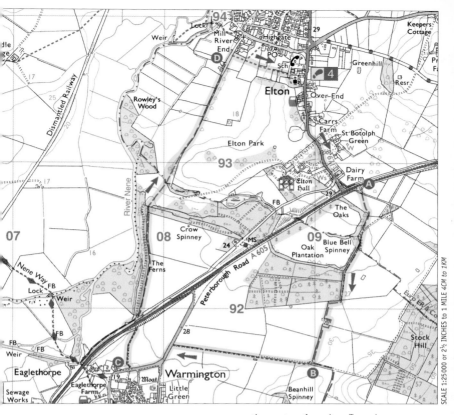

SCALE 1:25000 or 2½ INCHES to 1 MILE 4CM to 1KM

| 0 | 200 | 400 | 600 | 800 METRES | 1 |
| 0 | 200 | 400 | 600 YARDS | ½ | |

KILOMETRES
MILES

junction. Then, just after passing Dexter Way, turn off through a waymarked gate on the right **C**. Walk forward, mounting a stile to carry on at the field edge. Where it subsequently curves above a cutting, look for a kissing-gate from which a contained path drops back to the main road. Carefully cross to the continuation of the path opposite that leads through to a track.

Turn right and climb past a turning area to a bridleway signed off left through a gate. It rises below a communications transmitter to continue outside the field edge. Later slipping into the bordering woodland, maintain your forward direction above the Nene, which although close by is hardly visible through the trees. However, passing out through consecutive gates, there is a fine view across the park to Elton Hall. Bearing slightly right, head down to a bridge beside a gate.

The onward bridleway rises around the edge of thicket before running above a succession of large fields. Developing into a lane as it passes cottages, keep on a little farther to reach more houses on the right. Turn off over a stile beside a gate on the right immediately before them **D** and strike out across the meadows towards Elton church. Leave over a stile by a gate at the top, just left of the church and go right into the churchyard. Below the northwest corner of the tower are two Saxon wheel-headed gravemarkers, however, little else of its early fabric remains, as it was largely rebuilt in the 15th century and subsequently twice restored. Walk out through the churchyard to return to the start. ●

Wimpole Park

		GPS waypoints
Start	Wimpole Hall	🖉 TL 338 509
Distance	5 miles (8km)	Ⓐ TL 330 510
Approximate time	2½ hours	Ⓑ TL 330 525
Parking	Car park at Wimpole Hall (National Trust)	Ⓒ TL 338 524
		Ⓓ TL 352 524
Refreshments	Restaurant and café at Wimpole Hall	
Ordnance Survey maps	Landranger 154 (Cambridge & Newmarket), Explorers 209 (Cambridge) and 208 (Bedford & St Neots)	

Wimpole lies amidst the folds of the gentle hills that rise to the west of Cambridge, and this ramble around the park and neighbouring farmland exploits the views to the full. The 17th-century hall looks out over 60 acres (24.3 hectares) of formal garden, both well worth visiting at the end of the walk.

Begun in 1640, Wimpole Hall (National Trust, tel. 01223 206000) has been extended and remodelled over the centuries and has become Cambridgeshire's grandest country house. Much of its splendour is due to its last owner, Elsie Bainbridge, daughter of Rudyard Kipling, who restored the house after her husband's death and refurnished the main rooms. The park and gardens are no less impressive, and include the work of several noted gardeners including 'Capability' Brown and Humphrey Repton.

🖉 From the car park, walk around to the stable block entrance below the clock tower and go through a metal gate directly opposite, from which a path is signed to the hall. It leads past the church, rebuilt by the Yorkes around 1749 and containing many funerary memorials in the large family chapel, the only remaining part of the original building. Keep ahead, passing between the house and an imposing avenue that

runs due south for almost 2½ miles (4km). Carry on to a second gate leading out to the park. Follow the fence right to a ha ha Ⓐ, there going left to climb away between young lime trees along West Avenue.

Turning right through a kissing-gate at the top, follow a line of trees at the edge of a wood. Where the avenue finishes, look for a stile beside a gate into the wood from which a path leads to the right. After some 350 yds (320m), look for a narrower path off right. The short detour takes you back out to the park at the edge of a small lake, across which there is a view to a hilltop folly, the Wimpole Ruins.

Return to the main path and follow it on through the trees until you eventually reach a waymarked junction Ⓑ, just before a gate at the edge of the wood. Turn right along a broad track that runs the length of a narrow woodland strip and ultimately emerges onto a lane Ⓒ. Cross to another path into the trees opposite. Bear left as it forks and then

Wimpole Hall

go right on meeting a broader track. Breaking out into more open ground, it continues at the edge of fields, finally leading to a junction beside a couple of concrete reservoirs **D**.

Turn through a gap in the trees on the right, from which a path, signed to Wimpole, follows the field edge. Approaching the end of the hedge, a waymark directs you right along a short path. Emerging onto a field track, follow it right down the rolling hillside to Cobb's Wood Farm. Continue past the buildings and over a small bridge, forking right to pass in front of Keeper's Cottage. Meeting a lane at the end, go left to a stile on the right. Strike half-left across a couple of pastures to return to the car park at Wimpole Hall. ●

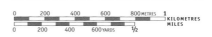

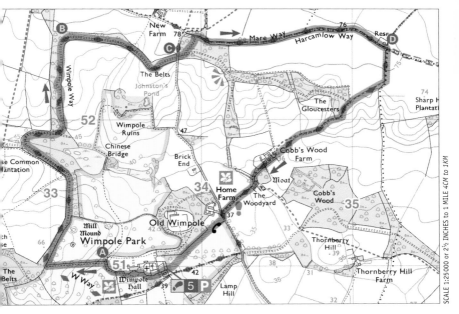

Horseheath and West Wickham

		GPS waypoints
Start	Horseheath	TL 611 472
Distance	4½ miles (7.2km)	**Ⓐ** TL 613 474
Approximate time	2 hours	**Ⓑ** TL 624 476
Parking	Roadside parking in the village	**Ⓒ** TL 621 489
Refreshments	Pub at Horseheath	**Ⓓ** TL 611 492
Ordnance Survey maps	Landranger 154 (Cambridge & Newmarket), Explorer 210 (Newmarket & Haverhill)	**Ⓔ** TL 608 482

Horseheath lies near the eastern border of Cambridgeshire, where the land puckers into lazy, rolling hills. The countryside is delightful and, as exemplified by this gentle ramble to the neighbouring village of West Wickham, offers a quiet and leisurely retreat.

The village takes for its emblem the racehorse Plenipotentiary, bred and trained here by Stanley Batson. Winning two races on his first day out at Newmarket in 1834, he subsequently won the Derby at Epsom and was again first at Ascot. The sign board also depicts the crowns of two monarchs that visited the village, Elizabeth I in 1578 and George V who reviewed troops here on exercise in 1912.

Begin from a junction by the tiny triangular green in the village centre and follow the lane towards West Wickham. Just before reaching the flint church take a path leaving over a footbridge on the right **Ⓐ**. Pass through an unkempt wood to a crossing of paths beside a kissing-gate and go left past paddocks. At the far end pass through thicket to the edge of an open field and turn left around its sinuous perimeter, eventually meeting a broad crossing track. Part of the same Roman road encountered on Walks 22 and 24, it ran from Colchester to Godmanchester. Follow it right for ½ mile (800m), passing the edge of Hare Wood.

At a junction of tracks at its far corner **Ⓑ** swing left beside the boundary, continuing beyond its end past the foot of Ash Plantation. As the accompanying hedge ends, a field track develops, but when this shortly bends right, keep ahead through a gap in the hedge. Bear right across the field, making for Hill Farm. Approaching the top, keep with the perimeter around to the left past the buildings to meet a

Down the fields to Streetly Hall

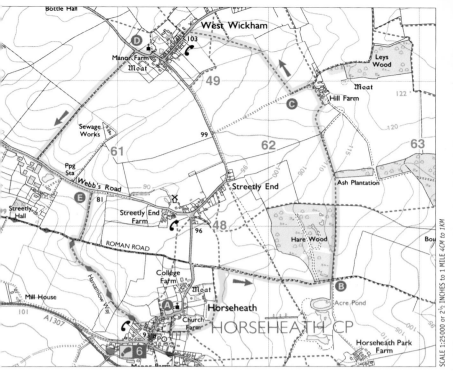

SCALE 1:25000 or 2½ INCHES to 1 MILE 4CM to 1KM

```
0    200   400   600   800 METRES  1
                                   KILOMETRES
                                   MILES
0    200   400   600 YARDS  ½
```

concrete access track. Go left.

After some 150 yds (137m) **C**, turn off right and follow a path directly away through the crop. At the bottom, a plank bridge spans the hedged ditch into the next field. Strike half-left, aiming for the distinctive gable end of a former chapel at West Wickham and continue the same line across a final field to emerge at its far corner in the village. Walk left to a junction and go right, winding past St Mary's Church. At the edge of the village, abandon the lane for a track off on the left signed as a footpath **D**.

It lopes gently downhill between open fields and affords a superb view across an undulating landscape broken by tracts of woodland, which give so much character to this corner of Cambridgeshire. Notice over to the left, the round tower of a disused windmill

at Streetly End. Crossing a stile, carry on between more fields to come out at the bottom onto a narrow lane opposite Streetly Hall Farm.

Go left, passing the estate entrance, but as the windmill tower comes into view ahead, leave for a field track marked as a footpath on the right **E**. Meeting another track at the far end, (the Roman road once more), walk right, but after crossing a ditched stream, turn off left onto a grass track that dogs its meandering course. The track later narrows to a path with a broad flowery margin, remaining with the stream to a footbridge over a side ditch. Just beyond, pass through a kissing-gate into the corner of a rough pasture and follow the hedge left. Leave through another kissing-gate at the far side and walk out between houses onto a street in Horseheath. Head right to find a footpath at its end, which winds out to the main lane by the start, with the Old Red Lion just to the right. ●

HORSEHEATH AND WEST WICKHAM ● 23

Reach, Swaffham Prior and the Devil's Dyke

Reach, Swaffham Prior and the Devil's Dyke

		GPS waypoints
Start	Reach	
Distance	4½ miles (7.2km) – 2¾ (4.4km) for short walk	✐ TL 567 661
		Ⓐ TL 564 662
Approximate time	2½ hours –1½ hours for short walk	Ⓑ TL 560 657
		Ⓒ TL 572 648
Parking	Car park at the corner of Fair Green, Reach	Ⓓ TL 567 639
		Ⓔ TL 572 649
Refreshments	Pubs at Reach and Swaffham Prior	Ⓕ TL 575 653
Ordnance Survey maps	Landranger 154 (Cambridge & Newmarket), Explorer 226 (Ely & Newmarket)	

Known variously as the Devil's Dyke or Ditch, this spectacular earthwork is Cambridgeshire's most prominent archaeological feature. The walk begins from its western end at Reach, crossing the fields to Swaffham Prior, unusual for having two churches occupying the same graveyard. The return is along the dike itself, giving fine views across the open landscape.

Reach's charter for a fair was awarded in 1201, and the size of the green, smaller than it once was, still testifies to a former importance. The village later developed as a busy port, with cargo travelling up the River Cam and along Reach Lode.

✐ From the car park, strike ahead across Fair Green to join the street leaving left from its far corner. Signed to Upware and the Devil's Dyke Walks, it twists right then left, at which point, go right along a short track marked to Reach Fen. After crossing a bridge Ⓐ, turn left and follow a track towards Spring Hall Farm, bypassing the buildings on their left to reach a lane.

Go left over a bridge Ⓑ, and then immediately turn off right onto a public byway, Barston Drove. A pleasant track, it curves around a low hill, giving a view across the fields to the churches and windmill of Swaffham Prior.

Reaching a lane Ⓒ, *you can shorten the walk by turning left,* otherwise follow it in the other direction. Keep going through the village, eventually passing the 18th-century Red Lion, the last survivor of Swaffham Prior's several pubs. Just beyond, turn off into the churchyard up a path Ⓓ past the front of the village's twin churches. Built to serve separate parishes, St Mary's is the older of the two, containing Norman stonework and still in use as a place of worship. Windows in the north aisle shine as the war memorial and look optimistically to a world of peace. The two parishes were amalgamated in 1667 and St Cyriac's is now in the care of the Churches Conservation Trust.

Swing left behind them to a stile and follow the onward path, passing a small green and shortly meeting a street. Cross to the continuation opposite, but after a few yards, detour right along a

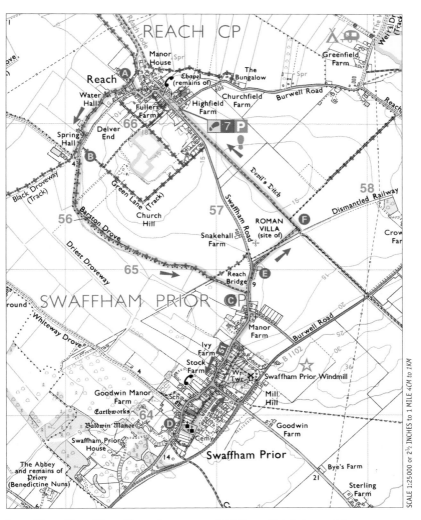

SCALE 1:25 000 or 2½ INCHES to 1 MILE 4CM to 1KM

```
0    200    400    600    800 METRES    1
                                         KILOMETRES
                                         MILES
0    200    400    600 YARDS    ½
```

rising grass path. Emerging in a small orchard at the top, bear left past the windmill to a drive and turn left back down the hill. Where it bends, keep ahead on a contained path that falls around the perimeter of a garden. Regaining the original path, follow it right, soon winding past sheltered housing to the main village lane.

Turn right, passing the point at which you first joined it **C** to find a concrete track 100 yds (91m) farther along on the

right. Immediately beyond it, a narrow path delves into the roadside trees **E**. Bear right to come out at the edge of a field and cut across the corner to a redundant gate. Drop into a disused railway cutting, climbing the opposite embankment a short distance to the right. Follow the field edge right at the top, the Devil's Dyke now a formidable sight in front. The path onto it dips first through its deep, defensive ditch, which is concealed by a clump of trees in the field corner.

Built around the beginning of the 7th century, it served to protect three

important routes into East Anglia against raids by British tribes. Running in a straight line for $7\frac{1}{2}$ miles (12km) and, at its highest, 34 feet (10.4m), it remains an impressive statement of Saxon power.

Gaining the top **F**, follow a path left along its crest. There is no obvious trace of the Roman villa that lay across the field to the left, but there is initially a grand panorama over the surrounding countryside. Cambridge lies to the south west whilst in the north west, beyond Wicken Fen, rise the distant towers of Ely's cathedral. Keep going as the path becomes hedged with bushes, passing through a couple of gates before finally emerging back at Reach onto Fair Green. ●

Swaffham Prior Windmill

Grantchester Meadows and Cambridge

		GPS waypoints	
Start	Grantchester		
Distance	6 miles (9.7km)	📍 TL 433 554	
Approximate time	3 hours	Ⓐ TL 438 568	
Parking	Street parking in Grantchester	Ⓑ TL 446 581	
		Ⓒ TL 448 585	
Refreshments	Pubs and tearoom at Grantchester, pubs and cafés in Cambridge		
Ordnance Survey maps	Landranger 154 (Cambridge & Newmarket, Saffron Walden), Explorer 209 (Cambridge)		

The rivers Cam and Granta combine their waters south of Grantchester, lazily flowing between meadows and lush woodland to the university city of Cambridge. Following its course, this relaxing walk offers a picturesque route to the colleges clustered at the city's ancient heart. Explore at leisure or perhaps take a punt on the river before returning along the bank to the village immortalised in Rupert Brooke's poem.

The son of a Rugby School master, Rupert Brooke attended King's College and settled in Grantchester in 1909, where he began writing poetry. Before the outbreak of war, he travelled widely and wrote *The Old Vicarage, Grantchester* in Berlin during 1912. But it was his war poems that brought him recognition. He enlisted in the Royal Naval Division, but his career came to a premature end with his death in April 1915 whilst en route to the Dardanelles. His body lies on the Greek island of Skyros and there is a memorial to him in the village church here. The Orchard Tea Room retains the quiet charm of that bygone age and its garden is a delightful place to unwind over afternoon tea.

📍 Follow the main street through the village north from the church, bearing right at a junction to pass The Rupert Brooke pub. Just beyond, leave through a kissing-gate on the right into Grantchester Meadows, the way signed to Cambridge. Strike across on a clear trod, bearing left where it splits and soon joining a tarmac path. To the left, it continues across successive meadows that run down to the river. Eventually becoming enclosed Ⓐ, it leads out to a track that develops into a leafy street.

At a fork before a small garage bear right and at the end of the street, go right again. Follow it left at the bottom, there looking for a kissing-gate on the right. A path delves into the rich woodland of Paradise Nature Reserve, winding beside a stream to join the river. Keep with it beneath pendulous boughs of willows, shortly leaving the main flow beside a leat. Emerging from the wood through a kissing-gate, pass a car park and then swing over a bridge to continue along the channel's opposite bank.

Reaching a main road, cross to resume the waterside path, which soon leads to a millpond overlooked by the former mill. Bear right across the meadows towards the river, following it to a bridge above a weir. Cross and walk out to the street beyond. Go left and then, as the street bends away, keep ahead along a narrow alley, Laundress Lane behind The Anchor pub to emerge on Silver Street **B**.

Turn back over the river and cross the road, swinging right past the corner of Queen's College to join a pleasant path largely set back from the main road. It leads past the college 'Backs': King's, Clare and Trinity Hall. Ignore the entrances to King's and Clare, but take the next pathway on the right,

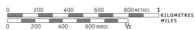

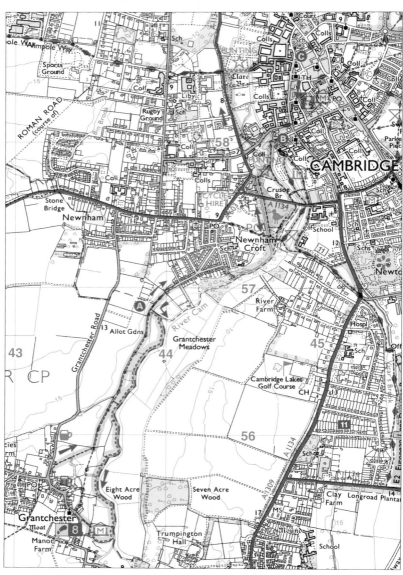

King's College Chapel, Cambridge

Garret Hostel Lane, which leads to a bridge across the river. Carry on between college buildings, turning left and then right into Trinity Lane. Walk up between Trinity and Gonville and Caius Colleges to Trinity Street at the top **C**. You are now in the pedestrianised heart of the city, the various colleges, churches and museums all within easy reach.

Cambridge has been a seat of learning since the beginning of the 13th century, when groups of students moved here from Oxford. Ever since the founding of the first college, Peterhouse in 1284, the university has influenced the character of this lovely city. Magnificent medieval architecture abounds in the college buildings and many churches, the best of all being the chapel of King's College, founded by Henry VI. Begun in 1446, it took almost 100 years to complete, and its exquisitely beautiful fan-vaulted roof portrays Perpendicular architecture at its finest.

The return follows Trinity Street to the right, passing the splendid King's College Chapel. Keep going along King's Parade to a junction overlooked by St Botolph's Church and turn right into Silver Street. Approaching The Anchor, go left back down Laundress Lane to the river, and retrace your steps to the edge of Grantchester Meadows **A**.

Varying the outward route, bear left at the end of the contained track to follow the meandering riverbank. Keep going for some 1¼ miles (2km) from meadow to meadow until eventually reaching a stile into a wood. Instead of crossing, follow the field edge away from the river round to a kissing-gate in the top right corner. Walk up to the main lane through the village and turn right back to the church. ●

Buckden and Offord Cluny

Start	Buckden
Distance	5½ miles (8.9km)
Approximate time	2½ hours
Parking	Roadside parking at Buckden
Refreshments	Pubs at Buckden, pub at Offord Cluny
Ordnance Survey maps	Landranger 153 (Bedford & Huntingdon), Explorer 225 (Huntingdon & St Ives)

GPS waypoints

🏁	TL 191 676
Ⓐ	TL 197 669
Ⓑ	TL 196 663
Ⓒ	TL 213 672
Ⓓ	TL 219 669
Ⓔ	TL 203 674

From Buckden, a gentle descent across fields into the valley of the Great Ouse is a preamble to a pleasant woodland path by Diddington Brook. The pools and meadows of a developing nature reserve flank the onward way to neighbouring Offord Cluny, from which the return is along quiet lanes.

Straddling the Great North Road, Buckden is dominated by a great palace, which was the residence of the Bishops of Lincoln for over eight centuries. The tower and gatehouse hint of a former extent and elegance fit to rival any regal palace and indeed it received many royal visitors. The most famed is that of Catherine of Aragon, banished here after she failed to produce a male heir for Henry VIII. However, she remained a favourite of the people and Henry grew nervous of her popularity and tried to get her removed to somewhere more austere and cloistered. Catherine's defiance and loyal supporters were more than a match for Henry's scheming and in the end she won the day, settling for relative comfort at Kimbolton.

The town's importance is also reflected in the parish church, where five Bishops of Lincoln are buried and the two great coaching inns that face each other across the main street, the George and the Lion. Variously known in the past as the 'Lamb and Flag' and the 'Lion and the Lamb', the Lion Hotel dates from the 15th century and originally served as a guesthouse for the

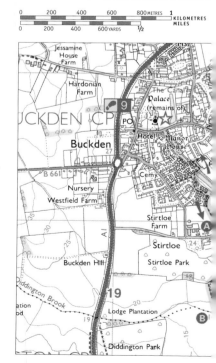

palace.

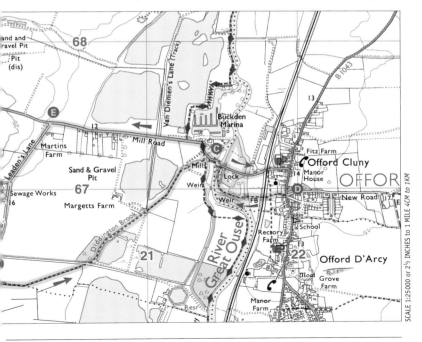 Begin from the junction by the Lion Hotel and leave along Church Street. Just beyond the church, turn right into Manor Gardens. Ignore a couple of junctions and then bear left on a bend. Pass out between the end houses onto a path in front of a tree-lined pool. To the right, bear left and right at consecutive forks, the path twisting through trees and over a bridge to emerge onto another street. Go left and keep ahead at an immediate junction. Rounding a bend look for a signed path between the bungalows on the left. Curving behind them, it runs away at the field edge to meet a lane **A**.

The path opposite follows the hedge bordering the field towards Diddington and grants an extensive panorama across the Great Ouse valley before it drops to a footbridge spanning Diddington Brook. Immediately beyond, turn left **B** along a signed path that dogs the stream. In time, the route becomes shadowed by the grassed embankments of extensive gravel workings to the right. Although obtrusive at present, this is a relatively temporary activity and leaves behind pools which, when allowed to naturalise, create valuable habitats for a wide variety of wildlife. The path eventually ends at a tarmac track.

Over a footbridge diagonally opposite, resume your course beside Diddington Brook passing woodland-fringed reedy pools, highlighting the recovery from seeming devastation. The way finally breaks into the open and leads to a gate. Cross a track and stile to continue by the hedged brook edging an open meadow towards distant buildings. Originally a flour mill, they have gained a new lease of life in conversion to housing. The path eventually swings across the brook and curves right to a kissing-gate onto a lane **C**.

You can shorten the route by simply returning along the lane to the left, otherwise turn past the mill buildings over bridges spanning the several arms of the river. Beyond a level crossing, the lane ends in Offord Cluny beside The Swan. The village's name derives from the fact that the manor was once held by the Benedictine Abbey of Cluny in France.

Go right past All Saints Church and then leave opposite New Road along a short track signed to the River Ouse and Buckden **D**. Bear left across the field behind, from which there is a fine view of the medieval church, to a white gate, where a traffic-light system warns of approaching trains. *Be careful crossing as there are four tracks and trains are fast and frequent.* Beyond another paddock, three bridges in quick succession take you back over the fragmented river. Meander on through trees to emerge past a lock onto the road.

Retrace your steps to the left beside the converted flour mills, continuing beyond the point at which it first joined it **C**. After passing Buckden Marina, Mill Road runs straight for $^1/_2$ mile (800m) to a junction **E**. Turn off into Leaden's Lane towards Stirtloe. At the edge of the village, the path along which you began the walk is signed off to the right **A**. Follow your outward route back into the centre of Buckden. ●

Buckden Towers and church

Stow cum Quy Fen

Start	Lode	**GPS waypoints**	
Distance	5½ miles (8.9km)	🖉	TL 533 627
Approximate time	2½ hours	Ⓐ	TL 530 626
		Ⓑ	TL 524 628
Parking	Considerate roadside parking near the church at Lode, not by the mill	Ⓒ	TL 514 626
		Ⓓ	TL 507 628
		Ⓔ	TL 507 624
Refreshments	Tearooms at nearby Anglesey Abbey	Ⓕ	TL 517 611
Ordnance Survey maps	Landranger 154 (Cambridge & Newmarket), Explorers 209 (Cambridge) and 226 (Ely & Newmarket)		

Farmed fenland landscapes come in many guises and here it is perhaps at its most attractive. The open fields are criss-crossed by tall hedge-lined droves, which, enhanced by several plantations and the open wooded pastures of Quy Fen give it more the character of parkland. The walk begins from the small village of Lode, near to the National Trust Anglesey Abbey, which makes a delightful visit to complete the day.

Although referred to as an abbey, Anglesey was only ever a priory, founded under the Augustinians in 1135. After the Dissolution, the estate passed through many secular hands and by the time it was bought by Huttleston Broughton, later Lord Fairhaven, and his brother in 1926, the house had undergone many changes. Fairhaven applied his great wealth to a startling transformation, creating not only a lavish country house but working a miracle in turning the unpromising surrounding fen into a masterpiece of garden and woodland. He was also a great patron of the arts and collected widely, amassing an amazing and varied collection of fine pieces from across the world. On his death in 1966, he bequeathed it to the National Trust.

🖉 Begin from the centre of the village by the church and post office,

opposite to which is a path beside a thatched house, signed to Lode Chapel. At the end, beyond the Baptist chapel, go right and left to skirt allotments, continuing beyond them along an enclosed path to emerge at Lode Mill Ⓐ.

The history of a mill on this site goes back to Domesday, with the present building dating from the 18th century. The mill worked until the 1920s, although in its latter years it was converted to grind burnt limestone to make cement. In the process of landscaping the grounds of the Abbey, Fairhaven had the mill preserved as a feature, which no doubt ensured its survival, with subsequent restoration returning it to full working order. Water-levels permitting, it operates on the first and third Saturdays of the month, the flour and meal produced

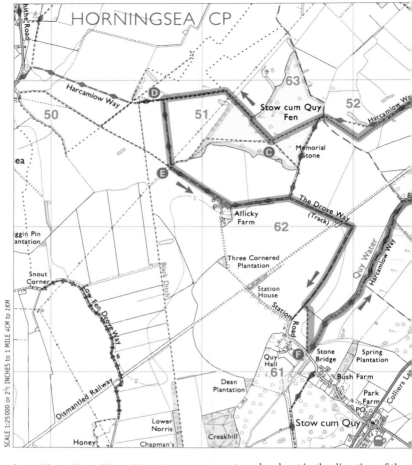

SCALE 1:25000 or 2½ INCHES to 1 MILE 4CM to 1KM

0	200	400	600	800 METRES	1
					KILOMETRES
					MILES
0	200	400	600 YARDS	½	

being available for sale.

Cross the stream and keep ahead at the perimeter of a field to the edge of a small wood, where another path goes off to the right within its boundary. At the end, turn left along the course of a dismantled railway and then shortly, go right on a hedge-lined way, (Dam Drove).

Swing left at the end **B** on another track. Keep ahead as the bounding hedges finish along a path beside a narrow ditch separating the fields, veering within the corner to reach a gated footbridge at the far side. Emerging onto the edge of a sprawling pasture, head out in the direction of the short, left-hand hedge, following a trod across towards distant trees. The trod leads to an obvious stile in the fence, but the one you want lies just a few yards to the right **C**.

Walk around the foot of a narrow reed-filled pond and follow its tree-shaded bank away to the right. At the far end, cross a stile on the right into the corner of a field and go left along its boundary. Cross a drain and keep going by the left hedge, now on a grass track. Reaching a copse on the right **D**, turn left at a waypost to then follow a field track. Reaching a junction of paths beside a pylon **E**, bear left with the main track along a wide, tree-lined drove.

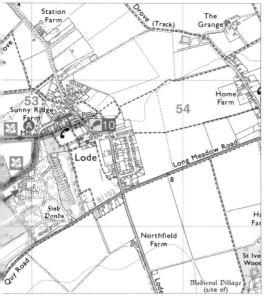

swings sharply right. After some 700 yds (640m), look for a kissing-gate by the corner of a hedge on the left. Entering a rough meadow, strike a diagonal across to another kissing-gate at the far side **F**.

However, do not pass through, instead double back left on a path topping the raised embankment beside Quy Water. It meanders pleasantly along giving splendid views over the fenland fields from its slightly raised vantage. Later passing into the woodland that surrounds Anglesey Abbey, there are glimpses through the trees of the house. Keep going past a bridge, soon returning to the mill and retrace your outward steps to the village. ●

Keep going with the main gravel track past Allicky Farm, remaining with it as it later curves right past a junction. At the next crossing, the main track bends away to the left, but keep ahead, now on a grass track, which soon

Reedy pool on Stow cum Quy Fen

Wicken Fen

Start	Wicken Fen, National Trust car park
Distance	6 miles (9.7km)
Approximate time	3 hours
Parking	National Trust car park
Refreshments	Tearoom at National Trust Visitor Centre, pubs at Upware and Wicken
Ordnance Survey maps	Landranger 154 (Cambridge & Newmarket), Explorer 226 (Ely & Newmarket)

GPS waypoints

🖉 TL 564 705
Ⓐ TL 559 711
Ⓑ TL 540 710
Ⓒ TL 536 701
Ⓓ TL 537 699
Ⓔ TL 571 701

Few areas remain to show what the fens looked like before they were systematically drained to create farmland, and that at Wicken is perhaps the best. The walk skirts the National Trust reserve to meet the River Cam at Upware, returning along Wicken Lode, a channel probably dug by the Romans. Keep your eyes open for koniks, which are related to the tarpan, a small wild horse from the Russian steppes and used to help manage the fenland vegetation.

Wicken Fen (telephone 01353 720274; www.wicken.org.uk) is the country's oldest nature reserve, acquired by the National Trust in 1899 to preserve something of this ancient and richly rewarding waterscape. An abundance of fish and waterfowl provided a living for early inhabitants, whose settlements were protected from both land and sea by the extensive marshes. This small area of wetland habitat still teems with life, the pools and channels full of invertebrates and fish. Dragonflies, damselflies and butterflies fill the air during early summer, whilst many waterbirds over-winter on the water. Other birds you might see include warblers, sparrowhawks and hen harriers and the list of plants and sedges is extensive. There are a number of hides within the reserve and the Visitor Centre contains interesting displays describing

the ecology and wildlife of the fen.

🖉 From the car park, go left

towards the Visitor Centre, but then almost immediately turn off right to follow Breed Fen Drove away from the lane. As the track later swings within the field corner, cross a stile just before a gate on the left Ⓐ. Head away along a raised bank, Spinney Drove at the edge of the reserve, continuing beyond it to emerge onto a lane, Upware Road. Cross diagonally right and strike out across the field opposite. Passing an encroaching corner, keep going beside the hedge, leaving through a gap at the far side onto a grass track Ⓑ.

Follow it left past a wood into another field. Turning right, then left, follow the edge around to remain within the field, paralleling the course of the as yet unseen River Cam. Through a kissing-gate just left of the far corner, cross a meadow to emerge over a footbridge onto a lane at Upware Ⓒ.

Go right and then wind left past the front of the Five Miles riverside pub, continuing, not on the grassy waterside sward, but remaining on the embankment above the river, marked Fen Rivers Way. Meeting another lane, turn right past a former pumping station towards a bridge across Reach Lode Lock, leaving left just before it along a path beside Reach Lode Ⓓ.

After crossing a footbridge over Wicken Lode, go left again, following the ancient channel bounding the Wicken Fen Nature Reserve. After a mile (1.6km) the waterway splits, the path bearing right beside Monk's Lode. Eventually reaching the edge of the fen Ⓔ, cross the drain at a gated bridge and turn right along a path towards the village of Wicken.

To reach the pub, keep ahead as it develops into a lane at the end. Otherwise, go left before the first of the houses following the field perimeter. Pass out through a kissing-gate part-way along and continue on a contained path that leads past the foot of a windmill. Carry on over a crossing drive, later joining a tarmac track. Eventually meeting a lane, turn left back to the car park. ●

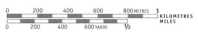

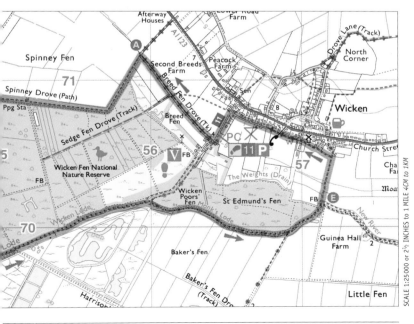

St Ives, Houghton and the Hemingfords

		GPS waypoints	
Start	St Ives	🖉	TL 314 712
Distance	6 miles (9.7km)	**Ⓐ**	TL 310 715
Approximate time	3 hours	**Ⓑ**	TL 281 722
Parking	St Ives	**Ⓒ**	TL 277 713
Refreshments	Pubs and cafés at St Ives, pub at Houghton, café at Houghton Mill, pub at Hemingford Abbots, pub at Hemingford Grey	**Ⓓ**	TL 283 709
		Ⓔ	TL 293 707
		Ⓕ	TL 312 710
Ordnance Survey maps	Landranger 153 (Bedford & Huntingdon, St Neots & Biggleswade), Explorer 225 (Huntingdon & St Ives)		

As I was going to St Ives, I met a man with seven wives ... so goes the old teaser which calls for a spot of lateral thinking rather than a mathematical bent to arrive at the correct solution. However, there is much more to dwell upon during this delightful ramble that explores the riverside meadows above the town and winds through picturesque villages of thatched cottages. Amongst the highlights are an 18th-century timber watermill, some fine churches and a Norman manor house as well as a delightful woodland nature reserve.

Taking its name from a Persian bishop, St Ivo whose relics were supposedly discovered here in 1001, St Ives was previously known as Slepe, from the Old English – a slippery landing place. It was the landing, however, that brought the town medieval prosperity. Granted a charter in 1110, its annual fair lasted a week and became one of the biggest in the country. The event attracted merchants from across the North Sea, sailing upriver to the quayside behind the market place. The fairs declined after the Black Death, which wreaked havoc on the population and was replaced by a weekly market that still takes place every Monday. The river trade from King's Lynn continued

to be significant into the 19th century, but that died with the advent of the railways.

The town is associated with several notable people, the most famous being Oliver Cromwell, to whom a statue stands in Market Hill. He was born in nearby Huntingdon but moved here to a farm in 1631. In our own time, Sir Clive Sinclair developed the world's first pocket calculator in the Old Mill, which stands across the river from the quay. Built in 1854 and powered by steam rather than water, the mill was owned by Potto Brown, whose statue you will encounter later at Houghton.

🖉 Standing back to back with Cromwell, walk along Market Hill and ahead past a junction. Beyond a riverside garden, where the street turns away Ⓐ, keep ahead on a path, signed the Ouse Valley Way, which leads into the churchyard of the parish church. Leave at the western end, passing a footbridge to continue along a tarmac path, Barnes Walk.

At a junction, keep ahead on the pleasant tree-lined path, which in time leads past The Thicket, an ancient woodland nature reserve. Beyond the wood, the way gradually develops as a lane, finally leading past large houses into Houghton. In the village square, The Green Ⓑ, there is an unusual thatched clock tower and a bust of Potto Brown, the wealthy mill owner and local philanthropist whose gift funded the Free Church at St Ives, but, pointedly, not its steeple, which he thought an extravagant ornamentation.

Leave left along Mill Street past St Mary's Church. At the end, swing left to the mill, and then turn right, passing through it to a bridge across the mill race. There has been a mill here since medieval times, originally owned by Ramsey Abbey, with the present building dating from the 18th century. During its peak, three separate wheels drove ten pairs of millstones and commercial production continued into the 1930s. Restored by the National Trust, it is the only example of a working watermill along the whole river.

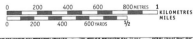

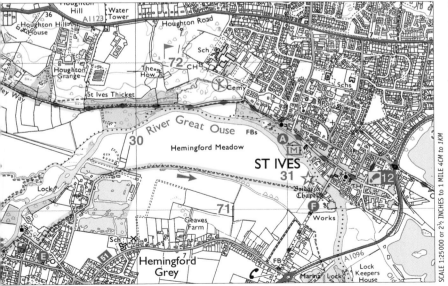

The ongoing path winds on to a bridge across a navigable reach above a lock. Strike out over the open expanse of Hemingford Meadow and across a final arm of the river. Keep ahead to meet the main lane in Hemingford Abbots **C**.

Turn left through the village and carry on past the Axe and Compass. Just beyond Manor Lane and a black-and-white cottage, Beechers House, leave left on a signed footpath **D** that leads beside a caravan site to the meadow behind. Strike across to the river, where a paths runs atop the raised flood embankment to the right. Joining a promenade, walk past Manor House to meet the end of a lane.

Instead of following the lane, go left on another signed footpath beside Riverside Cottage, which remains with the riverbank to a street by St James's Church. Head along the street for some 75 yds (69m) before turning off left into Love Lane **E**. Narrowing to a path, it leads behind houses and past the end of a street to meet a road. Cross to Meadow Lane opposite, signed as a footpath to St Ives. Beyond its end, pass through a kissing-gate onto the edge of Hemingford Meadow and follow a worn path at its edge.

The slender steeple of the parish church is seen ahead, shortly followed by that of the Free Church. Eventually the path curves towards the river, finally leaving through a kissing-gate in front of a rambling building, the Dolphin Hotel. Walk beneath a covered passage to gain the road **F** and turn over the bridge into the town. At the end, go right to return to Market Hill.

The elegant stone bridge striding across the river is one of only four remaining in the country that incorporates a chapel. When built around 1420, to replace an earlier timber structure, such features were not uncommon and served both as toll booths and places to hold services. During the Civil War, two of the arches were replaced by a drawbridge, to give better defence to the town should it be attacked by the Royalist army. ●

The Great Ouse at Hemingford Grey

Wansford, Sutton, Upton and Thornhaugh

		GPS waypoints	
Start	Wansford Bridge	🥾	TL 075 990
Distance	8 miles (12.9km)	Ⓐ	TL 077 995
Approximate time	4½ hours	Ⓑ	TL 094 987
Parking	Roadside parking in village	Ⓒ	TL 100 992
Ordnance Survey maps	Landranger 142 (Peterborough), Explorer 227 (Peterborough)	Ⓓ	TF 106 002
		Ⓔ	TF 098 005
		Ⓕ	TF 082 001
		Ⓖ	TF 073 005

After meandering through water meadows beside the River Nene to Sutton, the walk follows quiet lanes to Upton. The return favours higher ground, passing Sacrewell Farm and Country Centre to Thornhaugh before finally dropping through fields and old meadows back to the medieval bridge at Wansford.

A fine old bridge unites the two halves of Wansford, striding across the River Nene in a succession of graceful arches. Overlooking all is St Mary's Church, dating from Saxon times but with a later broach spire characteristic of the area. For much of its history the church was without a chancel and then claimed to be the smallest parish church in England, just 30 by 25½ feet (9.1 by 7.7m). Amongst its treasures is a beautifully carved Norman font, discovered at nearby Sibberton Lodge where it did duty as a cattle trough.

🥾 From the Haycock Hotel, cross Wansford Bridge and, at a junction by the church, go right. Just before the main road, look for a concrete track dropping right, marked as the Nene Way. Wind beneath the twin road bridges and climb to a picnic area Ⓐ. Walk through, joining the service road, but where it swings to the main road, leave right on the continuing Nene Way. Beyond a fringe of bushes, skirt an enclosure to a stile and wander down to the river.

Accompany the bank downstream through a succession of riverside meadows. After almost ¾ mile (1.2km), the path swings up between fences to run beside a wood. Follow the developing track until the way is barred by a gate, to the right of which is a kissing-gate.

The small church at Upton

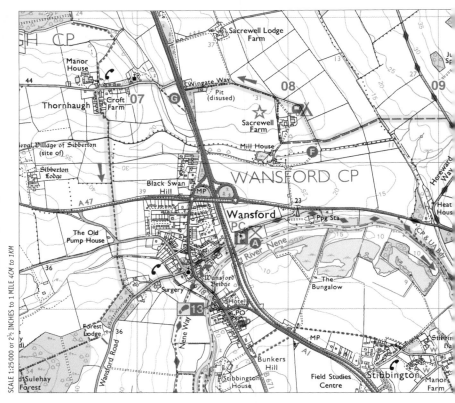

Slip through to continue in the adjacent field and then along an enclosed path, shortly meeting a lane in Sutton **B**.

Turn left past the 12th-century church and over a disused railway,

The River Nene

walking beyond the village to a T-junction. Go left to a roundabout on the busy main road **C**, carefully crossing to the continuing lane opposite. Signed to Upton, it rises gently through open countryside. Just before reaching Model Farm at the top of the hill **D**,

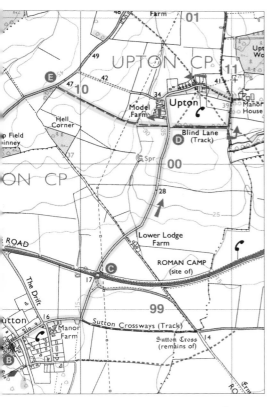

0 | 200 | 400 | 600 | 800 METRES | **1**
0 | 200 | 400 | 600 YARDS | **½**

KILOMETRES
MILES

fields and eventually reaching a lane **E**. Head left and then, at a junction, right, walking on for some 250 yds (229m) before leaving through consecutive waymarked gates on the left. Just ahead, turn through a field gate on the right, and follow the left-hand fence away. Entering a large crop field, bear left down to a foot-bridge, partway along the bottom boundary. Climb away with the hedge on your right, meeting a tarmac drive at the top **F**, which to the right, leads past Sacrewell Farm.

Skirt a camping field and then bear right between open fields. At a later fork keep left, shortly entering trees before meeting the A1 **G**.

Carefully cross the dual carriageway through a gap in the crash barrier and take the lane opposite into Thornhaugh. In the village, go left along Meadow Lane entering the field at its end. Follow the left perimeter down to a footbridge and climb away with a high hedge on your left.

Meeting a main road at the top, cross to a stile opposite and carry on across a sloping meadow. Emerge through trees at the bottom to a junction of lanes. Another footpath opposite drops through a kissing-gate across an old meadow. Over a bridge, head up beside a small plantation of saplings. Reaching the edge of a mature wood, look for a waymarked path into the trees. It winds through to Wansford Road, which to the left returns you to Wansford's church.

leave right through a gap into the field. Doglegging left, follow a grass bridleway that runs between trees and a hedge, Blind Lane. At the end, go left, soon emerging onto a metalled track by Manor House. Grassy mounds betray the site of the medieval village that surrounded the now isolated church, which was extended to accommodate the private chapel and lavish burial vault of the lords of the manor. Closer to, a curiously carved stone stands in a small paddock, an elaborate 17th-century sundial.

Turn left through the present village, keeping left again past Model Farm back to point **D**. Now, cross the stile on the right and accompany the fence away, continuing between subsequent

Stilton and Folksworth

		GPS waypoints
Start	Stilton	🖊 TL 162 893
Distance	6 miles (9.7km)	Ⓐ TL 158 893
Approximate time	3 hours	Ⓑ TL 150 878
Parking	Roadside parking at Stilton	Ⓒ TL 144 883
Refreshments	Pubs at Stilton, pub at Folksworth	Ⓓ TL 133 890
Ordnance Survey maps	Landranger 142 (Peterborough), Explorer 227 (Peterborough)	Ⓔ TL 147 899

From Stilton, the walk describes a pleasant circuit of the gently rolling countryside that lies just to the south of Peterborough. The route offers fine views and some attractive wooded stretches, and passes the not-unimpressive site of the deserted medieval village of Washingley and its motte-and-bailey castle.

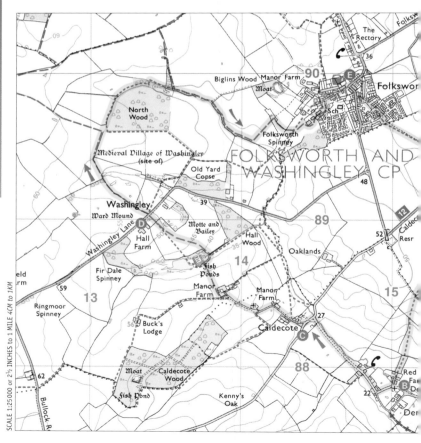

One of Britain's best-known cheeses takes its name from the village, yet perhaps surprisingly, it has never actually been made here. On Ermine Street, the Great North Road and a day's ride from London, Stilton was an important stage and mail post and, for 250 years, a focus of trade for the surrounding countryside. Amongst other produce, local farmers brought their cheese for sale in the market and the many coaching inns that once lined the main road. Tradition has it that the recipe for the rich and creamy blue-veined cheese was formalised in the early 18th century by a Mrs Pawlet, a former housekeeper at Quenby Hall in Leicestershire. Her brother-in-law, a Mr Thornhill and landlord of The Bell here in the village, served it to his guests and its reputation above the others was quickly established. Now protected by European regulation, it is made only in Leicestershire, Nottinghamshire and Derbyshire and just six dairies are licensed to produce the cheese. Thornhill was not only a successful business man but also famed for his riding skills and for a wager rode from his inn to London and back and then back again to London, covering a total distance of 213 miles (343km). He completed the epic journey in just over 12 hours to win his 500 guineas.

Almost opposite The Bell, weighed down by its imposing signboard, is Church Street. It leads away from the village centre past the church, dedicated to St Mary Magdalene. Where the road bends Ⓐ, keep ahead on a lane, which shortly degenerates to a track. At the end, just before a cottage, bear left to a stile and climb upfield to another stile. Maintain the same direction in the next field, crossing through a gap and plank bridge at the crest. Keep going along a cleared path through the crop.

Ignore a lateral track across the top and strike half-left to a stile in the bottom hedge. Carry on beside the right boundary, side-stepping a small pond to leave by a gate at the bottom. Pass along a narrow rough field to Red Hill Farm, walking through the yard to come out on a lane Ⓑ.

Follow it right, swinging right again past a junction in front of School Cottage to leave the hamlet. Reaching the end of the lane at the tiny neighbouring settlement of Caldecote, go left towards The Giddings. At a fork Ⓒ, bear right and follow the lane up to a converted Victorian chapel. Keep going on the continuing track to Manor

Thatched cottage near Stilton

Farm. Approaching the buildings, bear off to skirt around them on the left and continue on a grass track that falls beyond towards a wood. At the edge of the trees go right and then left across a ditch, passing through a fringe of trees to a gate. A swathe guides you on across a meadow, curving past a ditch and mound, which is all that remains of Washingley Castle. Leave through a gate, just right of Hall Farm and walk out between the impressive pillars of a stone gateway onto a lane **D**.

Cross to the bridleway opposite, which leads past the rambling site of Washingley medieval village, which lay in the fields to the right. Over a bridge, climb gently on to the top of the field. Turn right over a footbridge then go left over a second bridge at the corner of North Wood. Skirt the perimeter, later passing into the trees to wind over a couple of bridges before emerging at the edge of the subsequent field.

Turn right, continuing through a narrow spinney into a second field. Eventually reaching its corner, swing left to the top of the field and go through a gate on the right. Follow the boundary to the far side, leaving on a grass track that winds through successive gates to emerge onto a street in Folksworth. Walk down to a road, bear left and, on reaching The Fox, go right. At a junction with Washingley Lane **E**, turn right again, walking up 100 yds (91m) to find a signed path leaving on the left.

Pass between the houses to a junction of streets and bear right along Blackmans Road. Meeting Townsend Way, go right again, but then immediately turn off left onto another path that leads to the field behind. Strike half-left to a stile in the distant boundary and continue on a diagonal across the pasture beyond. Around you are traces of medieval strip ploughing and in front, the tower of Stilton's church. Reaching a road at the bottom, follow it left into the village. At the end go right and then swing left **A** to retrace your outward steps to the start point. ●

Lolworth, Knapwell and Boxworth

Start	Lolworth	GPS waypoints	
Distance	6 miles (9.7km)	🔖 TL 366 640	
Approximate time	3 hours	Ⓐ TL 355 617	
Parking	Roadside parking at Lolworth; please do not park on the Green	Ⓑ TL 333 624	
		Ⓒ TL 334 629	
Refreshments	Pub at Boxworth	Ⓓ TL 345 638	
Ordnance Survey maps	Landranger 154 (Cambridge & Newmarket), Explorer 225 (Huntingdon & St Ives)	Ⓔ TL 349 645	

This ramble over rolling countryside is completely delightful and makes use of old green tracks to link three quiet villages, while part-way round, you will find a pub at Boxworth.

For cars, Lolworth lies at the end of the road, but in the less-hectic days before the automobile, the lane carried on as a cart track between the fields to Childerley. Until the 17th century, there was a village at Childerley, but it was razed by Sir John Cutte to make way for a deer park. Charles I was briefly detained at the Elizabethan mansion in 1647 on his way from imprisonment at Holdenby Hall in Northamptonshire to eventual execution in London.

🖊 Beginning from the crossroads in the centre of the village, follow High Street in the direction of Childerley. The lane ends at a cottage but keep going on a broad grass track, which after a good mile (1.6km) leads to a gate. Pass

Knapwell's church

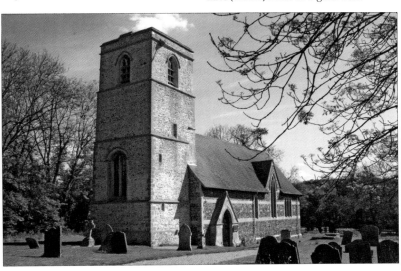

Along Thorofare Lane

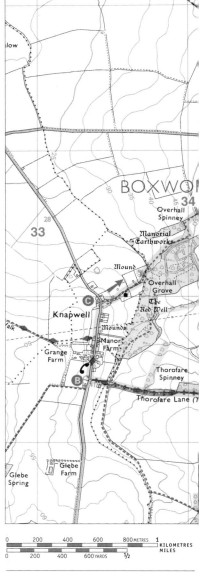

through into a rough meadow and continue beside the right hedge, bearing left at the far end to emerge through a gate at Childerley Hall Farm **A**.

Curve right to join a tarmac track, which winds away past the large sheds of a grain store. Carry on beyond them for another 100 yds (91m) before leaving through a waymarked gap in the left boundary. Walk away, with the dividing hedge on your left, keeping ahead in the field corner through a break in the hedged ditch. With the hedge now on your right, stride on, eventually joining a concrete track that leads out to Battle Gate Road. Cross and continue along the track opposite, Thorofare Lane, which ultimately ends onto a lane at the southern edge of Knapwell **B**.

In the woodland to the east of the village is the 'Red Well', whose waters were reputed to effect miraculous cures and it became regarded as a holy well. Whatever its medicinal properties, the well supplied the village with fresh water.

Turn right through the attractive linear village, leaving towards the far end along a track on the right signed to the Nature Reserve, Boxworth and

Knapwell Church **C**. Beyond the church, the track ends by a house, but keep forward on an enclosed path through trees. Over a footbridge, the path climbs into a field. The right of way initially hugs the right-hand boundary before crossing to the other flank to emerge onto a track at the top left corner. Cross diagonally left and continue on a field path, slipping

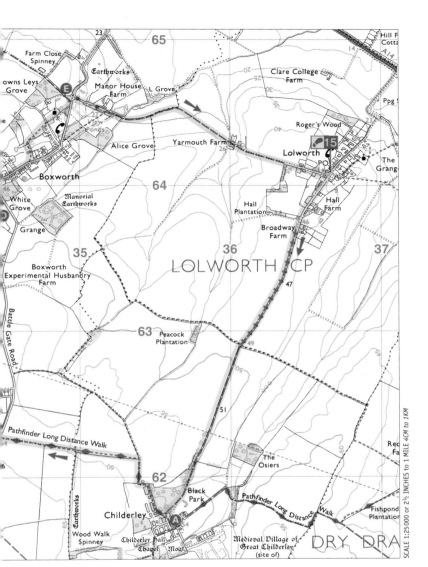

through a gap in the hedge towards the far end. Bear left to a kissing-gate from which a grass swathe conducts you out to a lane **D**.

Go left to meet the main lane opposite The Golden Ball and turn right into Boxworth. After some 300 yds (274m), leave through a kissing-gate on the left and strike out across pasture to a gate in the right corner. Continue in the subsequent field, bearing right towards its far end to find a small kissing-gate tucked around the corner.

Cross the end of a track into Boxworth churchyard and walk past the church, joining a drive that meets back with the lane. Go left and almost immediately right into Manor Lane **E**.

Where the tarmac ends, keep ahead between a couple of ponds. A broad green path carries on at the field edge, later curving gently right and leading to Yarmouth Farm. Climb away along its access track, which soon develops as a lane and takes you back into the centre of Lolworth.

●

St Neots and Little Paxton

		GPS waypoints
Start	St Neots, Riverside Park	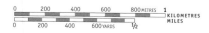 TL 179 601
Distance	7½ miles (12.1km)	Ⓐ TL 182 606
Approximate time	4 hours	Ⓑ TL 186 616
Parking	Riverside Park car park	Ⓒ TL 190 622
Refreshments	Pubs and cafés at St Neots, pub at Little Paxton and refreshments at Paxton Pits Nature Reserve Visitor Centre	Ⓓ TL 203 639
		Ⓔ TL 197 640
		Ⓕ TL 195 629
		Ⓖ TL 189 627
Ordnance Survey maps	Landranger 153 (Bedford & Huntingdon), Explorer 225 (Huntingdon & St Ives)	

Beginning from St Neots' spacious riverside park, the walk follows the River Great Ouse north to an extensive nature reserve that has grown up around the abandoned pits of sand and gravel workings. For those with time to spare, several marked trails explore the area in greater detail and the Visitor Centre contains a wealth of information on the reserve's history and wildlife.

Founded in 974, Eynesbury Priory stood on the east bank of the river, just north of the bridge, and brought prosperity to the town after the remains of St Neot, a monk from Glastonbury Abbey, were buried there. Abandoned at the Dissolution, there is now no trace of the monastery, but the memory of the saint was perpetuated when the town changed its name.

From the corner of the car park by St Neots Bridge, pass beneath and climb steps to the road. Cross the river and immediately turn off beside The Bridge House along The Priory. Take the next right, and then go left between car parks, past a cycle shed along the Ouse Valley Way. Cross a street at the far side and keep ahead down a passage, along Priory Road, and then a short track to reach a crossing drive Ⓐ.

Through the kissing-gate opposite, strike half-left across an open field to a gate and turn through into the adjacent Lammas Meadow. Lammas meadows were an important feature of medieval village economy, for although the growing crop was reserved for householders, commoners were allowed to graze their livestock on the stubble after Lammas Day, the traditional harvest. Head across to the River Great Ouse and follow the bank downstream. At the far end, a fence ushers you away from the river to a gate. Passing through, continue beside a ditch at the edge of Islands Common, eventually reaching a road Ⓑ.

Cross left at the junction, crossing to an elevated walkway that straddles the twin arms of the river. Gaining the far bank, turn right onto a tarmac path behind houses. Through gates carry on past a small housing estate and, where the path later swings away, walk forward over grass to a gate at the edge

0	200	400	600	800 METRES	1	
						KILOMETRES
						MILES
0	200	400	600 YARDS	½		

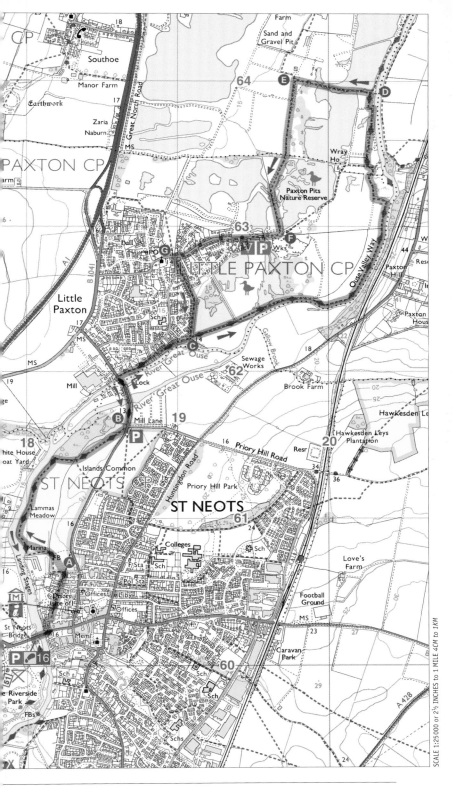

SCALE 1:25000 or 2½ INCHES to 1 MILE 4CM to 1KM

of the Paxton Pits Nature Reserve **C**.

Still marked 'Ouse Valley Way', a wooded path leads through the reserve, offering glimpses of the pools and later, the river. Keep ahead until the path splits at the edge of more open ground and take the lesser right-hand branch, which borders a rough meadow beside the tree-lined river. Reaching the far side, the path curves from the water to a crossing track. Go right, skirting a tangle of wetland wood. Shortly, a brief deviation is justified where a riverside viewpoint is signed off into the trees.

Returning to the main path, walk on to another fork and again go right. After passing moorings, a gate opens into more woodland. Carry on a little farther, but at the next junction **D**, leave the Ouse Valley Way and follow a path left.

Reaching the edge of a working gravel pit, continue past the yard to a waymark **E**. Turn left beside the service road and follow it away. Eventually leaving past a barrier turn right to the Visitor Centre **F**.

Beyond, as the road then forks keep left and continue along a residential street into Little Paxton. After passing The Anchor, take the second turning on the left, Gordon Road **G**. A few yards along, a gravel path branches left behind the houses. Later, bear right past a gate into the reserve and continue beside a lake to a junction where you first entered the reserve **C**. Turn right and retrace your outward route to St Neots.

The Great Ouse from St Neots Bridge

Isleham

		GPS waypoints
Start	Isleham	TL 642 743
Distance	7 miles (11.3km)	**A** TL 641 733
Approximate time	3½ hours	**B** TL 640 729
Parking	Roadside parking at Isleham	**C** TL 627 720
Refreshments	Pubs at Isleham	**D** TL 610 733
Ordnance Survey maps	Landrangers 143 (Ely & Wisbech) and 154 (Cambridge & Newmarket), Explorer 226 (Ely & Newmarket)	**E** TL 608 737
		F TL 623 744
		G TL 636 741

Beginning from Isleham, this walk wanders the fens that stretch as an apron to the west of the village. Much of the way follows the angularly aligned lanes and droves that fragment the marshes, as well as a section of a former branch line that ran to Mildenhall in neighbouring Suffolk.

Isleham grew from a small monastic settlement dependent upon the Benedictine abbey to St Jacutus in Brittany. It was suppressed in 1414 during the Anglo-French Hundred Years War and all that remains is the austere

priory church. The nearby parish church succeeds an earlier Saxon foundation and was built around 1330, with the high clerestory and splendid hammerbeam angel roof being added some 150 years later. The chapel in the south transept contains painted canopied funerary monuments to the

Isleham Priory

Peytons, whilst effigies of knights repose in the alcoves.

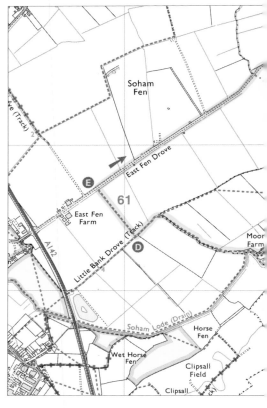

From the old priory, walk past the garage, turning right beyond the bend into West Street. At its end, go left along Hall Barn Road, and when that finishes, turn right on Fordham Road Ⓐ. After ¼ mile (400m), as the road begins to rise, fork off right on a short track Ⓑ that leads to a small parking area. Bear right to leave beside a barrier along a hedged grass track that once carried the railway.

Reaching here in 1885, the line primarily supplied farm produce to the markets in Cambridge and operated for three-quarters of a century. This short section has been retained as a nature reserve and amongst its many colonists is broomrape, which lives as a parasite upon other plants. Having no need of chlorophyll its dirty pinkish hue sometimes earns it the name of 'corpse plant'.

Where the track later opens out, stay with the path or alternatively walk in the adjacent conservation meadow, either way meeting the bend of a gravel farm track at the far side. Keep ahead at the field edge towards a high railway bridge, at the foot of which, go left beside the buttressing embankment to emerge onto a lane, Fordham Moor Ⓒ.

Follow it over the bridge and on past New Farm, eventually

Hall Farm

reaching Moor Farm at its end. Walk through the gate ahead and past a barn swinging left behind it. The track, marked as a footpath, winds away, initially beside an embanked stream, Soham Lode. Remain with the track as the stream moves away, continuing beyond its end along the left-hand edge of a large pasture. Arriving at the corner, pass out over a stile and bear left through a copse. Emerging, the path continues between a rampant hedge and a largely unseen drainage ditch on the right. After 250 yds (229m), look for a footbridge over the ditch **D** and head away at the subsequent field edge to a narrow road bounding its far side **E**.

Turn right, remaining with it as it later bends sharply right past a

junction. At the next junction **F**, go ahead on a narrower lane that plots an angular course around the perimeter of expansive fields. Eventually reaching a sharp right-hand bend on the edge of Isleham **G**, take the gated track in front marked as a footpath towards Hall Farm. Where it swings left to the house, continue on a grass path, crossing a drive to pass a large paddock. Emerging onto a back lane, walk forward to the next bend, there leaving along another waymarked path. Through a kissing-gate at the end, bear right across the corner of rough grazing to return to the village centre beside the priory. ●

Willingham and the Great Ouse

		GPS waypoints
Start	Willingham	 TL 404 704
Distance	6 miles (9.7km)	**A** TL 405 711
Approximate time	3 hours	**B** TL 417 728
Parking	Roadside parking at Willingham, near the church	**C** TL 437 721
Refreshments	Pubs at Willingham	**D** TL 421 700
Ordnance Survey maps	Landranger 154 (Cambridge & Newmarket), Explorer 225 (Huntingdon & St Ives)	

*This walk along fen droves and beside the River Great Ouse
begins from the village of Willingham, once on the pilgrims' way
to Ely. The church is famed, amongst other things, for its wall
paintings, which span a period of some 400 years and portray
a variety of subjects, which the priest would use to illustrate
his teachings.*

[👣] Start from a junction on the main road near the church and walk north along George Street. Keep with it around a bend and continue to the edge of the village where Flat Road, a track marked as a bridleway, leaves on the right **A**. Soon swinging left it heads out between the fields. Reaching a concrete track, go left and shortly veer right with it, passing

Looking across the fens

Flat Road Farm before approaching the River Great Ouse at Flat Bridge.

As the track rises to the bridge **B**, leave and climb to a kissing-gate on the right, from which a meandering path follows the ridge of the flood embankment above the river. There are open views across the fens, whilst closer too occasional wooded glades on the narrow flood meadow provide cover for small birds and waterfowl. Keep going past Queenholme Farm, in time arriving at a kissing-gate beyond which the embankment is broached by a track **C**.

Follow it away from the river between expansive fields, the grass way shortly joined by a prominent track. Where that then binds right, keep ahead as the grass track resumes, walking for another ³⁄₄ mile (1.2km) to meet a lane. Again, follow this forward for a short distance, but where it bends walk on along the continuing track. The hedged way finally ends onto a lane, Iram Drove **D**.

To the right, it eventually leads to Willingham. Go forward when you reach a crossroads, soon returning past the church to the start point. ●

Ely and Little Thetford

		GPS waypoints
Start	Ely Tourist Information Centre	TL 537 802
Distance	7 miles (11.3km)	**A** TL 539 798
Approximate time	3½ hours	**B** TL 533 787
Parking	Ely	**C** TL 530 764
Refreshments	Pubs and cafés at Ely	**D** TL 536 757
Ordnance Survey maps	Landranger 143 (Ely & Wisbech),	**E** TL 544 793
	Explorer 226 (Ely & Newmarket)	**F** TL 544 798

Once a remote island deep in the marshes, Ely's fascinating history justifies a visit in its own right. This pleasant walk across the fields to Little Thetford returns along the banks of the River Great Ouse and reveals the character of today's surrounding landscape, yet leaves ample time to explore the cathedral and discover something of the town's past.

Ely's story begins in the 7th century with the founding of a double monastery by Ethelreda, a Saxon princess. After the death of her first husband, who gave her the island, she married Ecgfrith, the future King of Northumbria, but then turned her back on secular life and retired to a nunnery at Coldingham. Her piety attracted a following and in 672 she established a small community of monks and nuns on the island. She ruled as abbess until her death seven years later, but her reputation persisted and the place eventually became a focus of pilgrimage. The austere Benedictine rule demanded both physical labour and spiritual devotion and the monks became celebrated for their singing. A fragment of an 11th-century ditty has survived, recalling a visit by King Canute:

'Merrily sang the monks of Ely,
As Canute the King rode by.
Row nearer the land knights,
And let us hear these monks sing'

But the Norman invasion clouded such carefree days, the tide of conquest being resisted in many places. Perhaps the most famous rebel was Hereward, a Lincolnshire thane who passed from history into myth after holding out at Ely against William's forces. Immortalised in Charles Kingsley's 19th-century novel, he had sacked Peterborough Abbey in protest against the appointment of a Norman bishop. When defeat seemed inevitable in 1071, he vanished into the fens and whispered stories of his subsequent exploits fanned the sparks of a legend.

The Normans consolidated their position with a motte-and-bailey and in 1080 began a new cathedral, which became known as the 'Ship of the Fens'. It is a truly impressive building with a nave the fourth largest of any English cathedral. A beautifully painted wooden ceiling is carried on soaring pillars, but even more magnificent is the unique octagon and lantern soaring above the transept. Replacing the original central tower that fell down in 1322, it is a feat

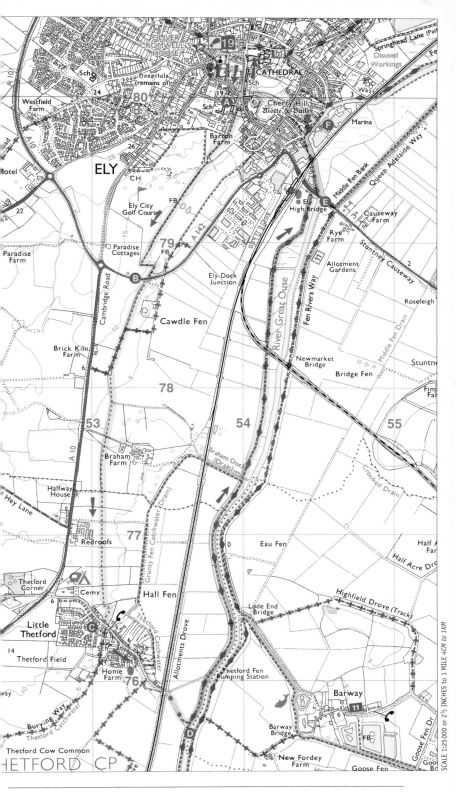

Ely Cathedral

of medieval ingenuity and craftsmanship. Tragedy struck again in the 15th century with the collapse of the northern aisle, bringing down with it the ornate façade and turrets flanking the western portal. Impressive too are the Bishop's Palace and buildings that became the old grammar school founded by Henry VIII, which incorporate a fine old gateway, known as the Ely Porta.

Leaving the Tourist Information Centre, for a time home to Oliver Cromwell, bear right past St Mary's Church to the cathedral. In front go right along The Gallery and over a mini-roundabout to a small triangular green. Cross ahead to a drive, marked as a footpath and leading to the King's School visitors' car park **A**. As it turns, keep forward, the way signed to Little Thetford, across playing fields and an assault course, and defined by occasional wayposts. Curving left at the far side, pass through a gate onto a golf course.

Bearing right, the onward path, confirmed by sporadic markers, strikes a beeline between the greens. Reaching the other side, follow a hedge left to cross a ditch and then swing right beside a final tee. Leave through a clump of trees onto a busy road **B**.

Carefully cross to a half-hidden footpath, just right of the entrance drive to Ely Water Treatment Works. Skirt the tree-lined perimeter of the plant, joining a track through a gate. Continue forward along a narrow copse dividing the fields. Where the track ultimately swings right, keep ahead into the corner of a field and carry on by the hedge.

Eventually, over stiles, go over a track to Braham Farm, maintaining your direction across a narrow meadow beyond to a kissing-gate. The way continues in an almost straight line through successive fields, later crossing another track by large agricultural buildings. Finally reaching a playing field, bear left towards a small wood, where a gap leads into the trees. A path runs to the left before turning beside a fence, soon leading to a gravel track. Follow it out to the lane in Little Thetford **C**.

Turn left, passing the small church dedicated to St Andrew, its plain interior brightened by an old octagonal font, four faces of which bear protruding carved heads. At the far end of the village, carefully cross an unmanned level crossing where lights warn of coming trains. A track winds on between the fields to the River Great Ouse **D**. Climb onto the embankment and, over a stile, follow it left towards Ely. After one mile (1.6km), the path crosses a bridge spanning a broad ditch, known as Braham Dock.

Continue by the river, later crossing another railway line. Carry on along the top of the dike, eventually leaving the fields behind to pass a sports ground. Emerging onto a road **E**, cross to the continuing waterside path and keep on past boat moorings and then beneath a railway bridge. Remain with the pleasant riverside walk as it swings below the Cutter Inn, turning away just beyond **F** to go through Jubilee Park. Reaching the road, cross to a gateway opposite, from which a path winds through Cherry Hill Park, giving a splendid view of the cathedral and passing below the site of the castle. Leave at the far side through the Ely Porta and, turning right, retrace your steps to the start. ●

Wimblington and Stonea Camp

		GPS waypoints
Start	Wimblington, by the church	
Distance	7¾ miles (12.5km)	🖊 TL 415 920
Approximate time	4 hours	Ⓐ TL 419 920
Parking	Roadside parking at Wimblington	Ⓑ TL 429 935
		Ⓒ TL 436 945
Refreshments	Pub at Wimblington	Ⓓ TL 446 942
Ordnance Survey maps	Landranger 143 (Ely & Wisbech),	Ⓔ TL 447 937
	Explorer 228 (March & Ely)	Ⓕ TL 527 809
		Ⓖ TL 416 931

Vast fields geometrically bound by ditches characterise the flat Fen landscape. But the scene is far from bleak and hedges bounding the droves linking the scattered farms break the view's emptiness. This walk leads to the impressive earthworks of Stonea Camp, an Iron Age settlement subsequently occupied by the Romans.

🖊 Begin along Chapel Lane, a cul-de-sac beside St Peter's Church at the southern end of the village and carefully cross the A141 to Manea Road. Beyond the houses, turn off left along a marked byway, Workhouse Drove Ⓐ.

Keep ahead as it develops into a green track, occasionally rough, but pleasantly hedged. Emerging onto Hook Road, follow it right for a little over ½ mile (800m) to a sharp right-hand bend Ⓑ. Leave there, continuing ahead

Embankments of Stonea Camp

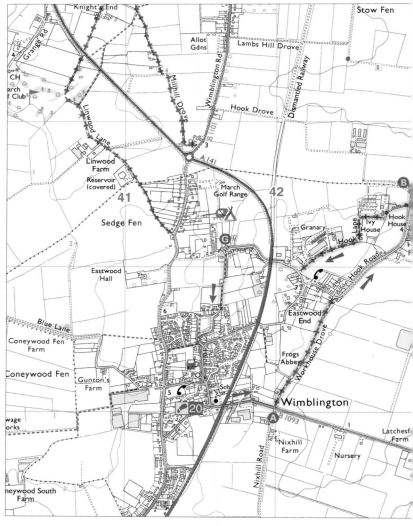

past Corner House on a bridleway, Firelots Drive. Towards the end, it abruptly veers right and runs out to a lane opposite Englands Farm **C**.

Go right but just before the farmhouse turn left through a gate. A path heads away at the field edge for a good ½ mile (800m) to meet a crossing field track **D**. Follow it right, swinging left at its end to a concrete farm road. Walk left past a house, but then after a further 50 yds (46m) **E**, strike across the narrow field on the right to a concrete bridge, marked by a footpath post visible from the road. Cross and

take a path beside the drain to the left. As it rises past a clump of trees, look for a stile on the right giving access to the Roman camp. There is a good overall view from the embankment, which curves left past a series of information boards to a stile at the far side **F**.

Once the Romans had quelled Iceni opposition, they colonised the Fens and established a town just north of the embanked camp, the only one known in the area. The site was occupied until the 4th century, and archaeological excavation has unearthed traces of a comfortable lifestyle including jewellery,

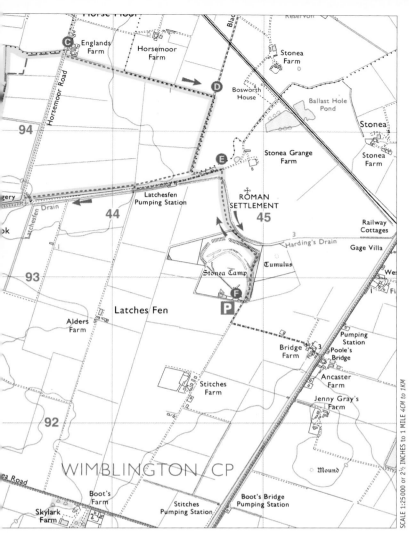

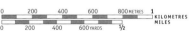

SCALE 1:25000 or 2½ INCHES to 1 MILE 4CM to 1KM

exotic foodstuffs and furniture preserved in the waterlogged ground.

Return to point **E** and follow the track left for ¾ mile (1.2km) to a lane at its end. Go left, eventually meeting your outward track at **B**. However, 100 yds (91m) after the bend, take the first turning right to Chapel Cottage Plants. At the end, bear left in front of the greenhouses along a grass byway. Skirting the nursery it then angles between fields, passing a rambling granary before meeting a lane. Go right to the main road and cross to the truncated Bridge Lane opposite.

Wind past houses for 350 yds (320m) and look for a signed path on the left **G**. It leads beside a paddock to a footbridge, doglegging over and swinging left along a hedged track to enter a small housing estate. Bear left around an open green and go left again at the far corner to a T-junction. Turn right into the old heart of the village, passing The Anchor and a row of thatched cottages. At the end, keep ahead along Church Street to return to the start. ●

Sawtry and the Giddings

		GPS waypoints	
Start	Sawtry, St Judith's Lane car park, first road off main street south of post office	🖊	TL 170 828
		Ⓐ	TL 166 822
Distance	7¼ miles (11.7km)	Ⓑ	TL 152 818
Approximate time	4 hours	Ⓒ	TL 139 809
Parking	St Judith's Lane, Sawtry	Ⓓ	TL 133 813
Refreshments	Pubs at Sawtry, tearoom at Little Gidding	Ⓔ	TL 126 817
		Ⓕ	TL 131 819
Ordnance Survey maps	Landranger 142 (Peterborough), Explorer 227 (Peterborough)	Ⓖ	TL 145 827

The walk climbs away from Sawtry through a tract of ancient woodland before crossing the pleasant and undulating landscape fringing the great fenland expanse of the Bedford Levels. It leads through the tiny hamlets of Steeple and Little Gidding, where small churches and a tearoom give excuses for a brief halt.

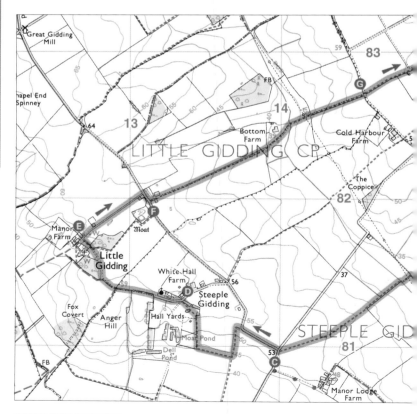

From the car park stile, climb away past allotments. Through a kissing-gate at the top, keep on at the edge of fields over the brow of a hill before dropping beside Aversley Wood. Immediately before a bridge at the bottom of a dip turn through a gate into the trees **Ⓐ**.

A broad drove strikes into the heart of the wood to end below a pool. Go left and, reaching a crossing by a bench, take the narrower path that runs on ahead. At a T-junction turn right and then later left, finally emerging over a stile beside a gate at the top edge of the wood.

Aversley is one of the largest single areas of woodland in Cambridgeshire and may be a remnant of the country's original forest cover. However, that does not mean it has been left to its own devices and over the centuries has

been managed to produce wood for a variety of purposes. Whole trees produced building timbers, while others were regularly coppiced to give poles, which could be used for fencing, tool handles and charcoaling. Indeed, some parts of the wood are still coppiced in the traditional manner. Native trees shade an under-storey rich in flowers, with bluebells and woodrush dominating early in the year. Other flowers appear later in their season, such as lords and ladies and the common spotted orchid. Foxes, squirrels and muntjac deer are never far away and in spring you may hear a woodpecker drumming.

Follow a track to the right, continuing beyond the corner of the wood. In time, reaching a waymarked junction **Ⓑ**, turn

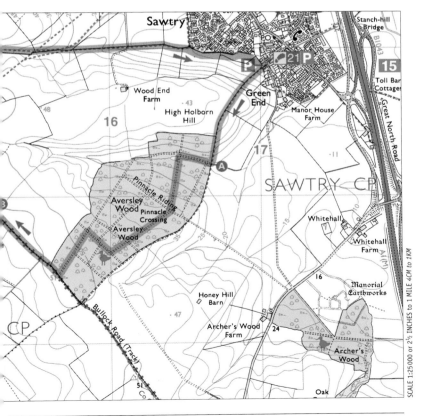

Steeple Gidding's church

Go left past the now-disused church of Steeple Gidding, which overlooks the fields where its village once lay. Approaching a wood, skirt it on the right to reach neighbouring Little Gidding . The church is to the left beyond a small car park, its narrow aisle and chancel lined with stalls and warmly panelled in wood. Nicholas Ferrar settled here in 1625, renouncing wordliness to establish a community of godliness. The place so impressed the poet T.S. Eliot when he visited in 1936 that he used it for the last of his *Four Quartets*.

Follow the lane away to the right. At the end go right, but leave after 100 yds (91m) through a gate on the left ❶. Beyond farm buildings, continue across fields, dipping past a small wood and eventually rising to a lane ❷.

Take the field path opposite to come out onto a track running at the far side. Bear right towards the gate of Woodfield farmhouse, but swing off left in front of it. A waymarked path follows a ditch and hedge away to the east, using a succession of footbridges to swap flanks three times. Eventually reaching a corner where a fourth bridge lies to the right, cross and then go left to walk with a different ditch now on your left. Reaching a dirt track, cross and continue by a hedge, later passing behind houses on the outskirts of Sawtry. Finally breaking from farmland, keep ahead across a playing field to return to the car park. ●

left down to Grange Farm. After passing the buildings, wind right and left to follow the access drive away. A short distance after rounding a sharp bend, take a grass track on the left. Over a drain, dogleg right and left to gently climb along the grass margin between open fields. Cross a bridged ditch at the top and maintain the same direction in a large arable field to come out onto a junction of lanes ❸.

Take the one ahead towards The Giddings. At a bend, drop into the corner of the field on the left and walk away beside a ditch. Turn across a footbridge and accompany the bottom hedge, swinging within the far corner to climb back upfield to a stile. Strike a right diagonal across the adjacent meadow, passing a small pond thick with reed mace to meet a lane ❹.

Linton, Hildersham and the Roman road

		GPS waypoints
Start	Linton, by the bridge across the River Granta	TL 560 468
Distance	7 miles (11.3km)	**A** TL 568 479
Approximate time	3¾ hours	**B** TL 576 490
Parking	Roadside parking at Linton	**C** TL 548 505
Refreshments	Pubs at Linton and Hildersham	**D** TL 549 492
Ordnance Survey maps	Landranger 154 (Cambridge & Newmarket), Explorer 209 (Cambridge)	**E** TL 543 484

Although hilly by Cambridgeshire's standards, the gradual gradients of this walk should present little difficulty to most people. It climbs from the ancient town of Linton over Rivey Hill to a Roman road, returning by way of Hildersham, where there is an interesting church, along the valley of the River Granta.

Linton's charter dates from 1246 and it remained an important market town until the mid-19th century. It has several fine part-timbered buildings, including the Bell Inn and the medieval Trinity Guild Hall, which stands to the north of the 13th-century church. There are also a number of cottages with façades decorated in attractive plasterwork.

From the bridge across the Granta, follow the main street east through the village, keeping ahead against the one-way system. Reaching a junction with the B1052, go left and then, first left again. Leave after 200 yds (183m) along a tarred path on the right, a bridleway to Balsham. Passing the cemetery, it later climbs at the edge of Rivey Wood, breaking out by a water tower **A**.

Descend the far side of the hill to a lane and keep ahead past the entrance to Chilford Hall Vineyard. Abandon it a little farther on, slipping through a gap in the right-hand hedge, from which a path, again signed to Balsham, diverges from the lane. Cross two fields, emerging through the top hedge onto the Roman road **B**.

Follow it left, shortly recrossing the lane to

Granta Valley near Hildersham

continue along the undulating tree-lined route. During the Middle Ages, wool-laden packhorse trains used the track and it became known as Wool Street. The Roman-sounding 'Via Devana' only appeared during the 18th century, when it was thought that the road led all the way to Deva, modern day

Chester. After crossing a second lane, carry on for a further mile (1.6km) until the track falls gently to a junction **C**.

To the left, a path signed to Hildersham falls between the fields. Meeting a lane **D**, walk along it right to a crossroads and go straight over, dropping past the church. Greatly restored during the 19th century, the chancel walls are richly decorated with colourful murals. Continue across the River Granta to the Pear Tree, turning left immediately after along a short lane signed as a footpath to Linton **E**.

Keep ahead where it finishes into a field, shifting right to a gate in the far corner. Follow the perimeter left, continuing over a track beside successive fields. Where the path forks soon after passing a water treatment plant, bear left, and continue to Little Linton Farm. Through a kissing-gate opposite, carry on between paddocks, eventually reaching the village recreation ground. Join a tarmac path along its edge, emerging at the far side onto a short street. At the end, go left back to the bridge spanning the River Granta. ●

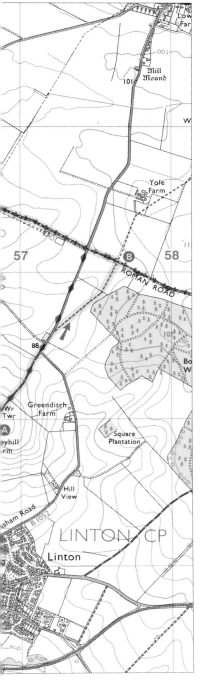

View from Via Devana

Castor Hanglands

		GPS waypoints
Start	Castor, in main street opposite the church	TL 123 984
Distance	7 miles (11.3km)	**A** TL 126 990
Approximate time	3½ hours	**B** TL 130 997
		C TF 128 002
Parking	Roadside parking at Castor	**D** TF 130 003
Refreshments	Pubs at Castor and Ailsworth	**E** TF 124 019
		F TF 122 023
Ordnance Survey maps	Landranger 142 (Peterborough, Market Deeping & Chatteris), Explorer 227 (Peterborough)	**G** TF 117 024
		H TL 117 988

Castor Hanglands is a protected area of woodland and heath overlooking the Nene Valley west of Peterborough. This walk to it begins from Castor, an important place in Roman Britain, climbing past its uniquely dedicated church to wind through a chequer of cultivation and copse.

Castor's church stands upon the site of one of the largest buildings known from Roman Britain, which extended over eight acres. The palatial villa was first excavated in the 19th century by Edmund Artis. He began life as a London confectioner and ended up as Steward to Lord Fitzwilliam of Milton, in whose employment he developed interests in natural history and archaeology. Occupied from around AD250 until the end of the Roman occupation, the extensive estate overlooked Durobrivae, a strategic town which grew where Ermine Street, the road from London to Lincoln, crossed the River Nene. The town was also the centre of an extensive pottery industry in the valley, producing a distinctive style known as Castor Ware. Served by roads and the river, it was exported around the country and pieces have been discovered in Wales.

Walk east (in the direction of Peterborough) along Castor's main street below the church. Turn left beside

the Royal Oak into Stocks Hill, which climbs past the end of the churchyard. The church is the only one in the country dedicated to St Kyneburgha, the daughter of the Mercian King Penda, who, widowed around AD650, founded a nunnery within the abandoned Roman ruins. After her death a cult developed around Kyneburgha's memory and her enshrined remains became a focus of medieval pilgrimage.

At the top of the lane, go forward on a track that soon narrows as an enclosed path to the main A47 road **A**. Carefully cross and, swinging left and then right, head away along a bridleway, Cow Lane to a junction at its end **B**.

Go left and continue through a gap into the next field. Where the track later curves left, leave beside a waypost on the right between open fields. Reaching the corner of a plantation **C**, turn right beside it on a hedged grassed track.

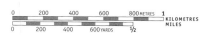

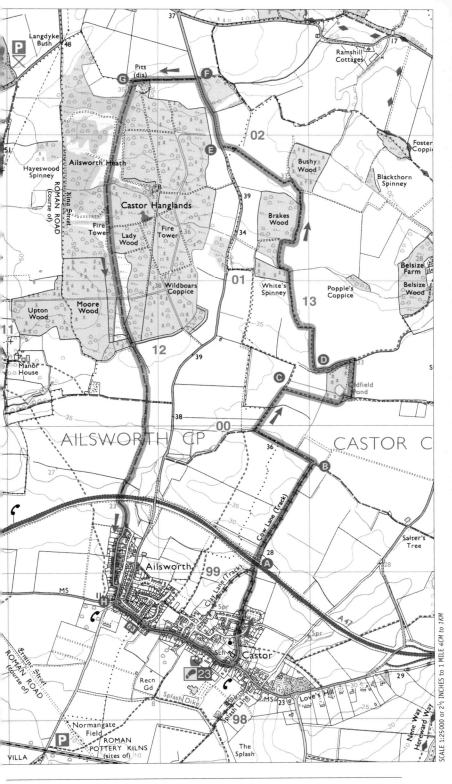

Later curving left to a junction, keep left and remain at the edge of the trees. At the next corner, by a sign to Castor Hanglands, turn left once more to perambulate the third side of the wood. Immediately after passing through a metal barrier **D**, swing off right along a broad swathe, which later doglegs left and right towards the corner of White's Spinney.

Just before the trees, slip through a gap in the accompanying hedge to continue past the eastern end of the wood. Follow the convoluted boundary to the top corner of Brakes Wood and strike ahead towards Bushy Wood. Turn left along the perimeter, going left again at a junction and head out between the fields to a lane **E**.

Walk right for ¼ mile (400m), as far as a bridleway on the left **F**. Initially at the field edge, it then borders a wood. At the end of the fence by a Natural England sign, 'Castor Hanglands National Nature Reserve' **G**, go left, following a path that leads through a gate into the woodland. Clearly waymarked, the ongoing route heads generally south through a succession of gates, belts of trees alternating with more open areas of grazing meadow.

A remnant of ancient woodland bounded to the west by the Roman road of King Street, the Hanglands were included within the medieval hunting forest of Nassaburgh. The open areas of the heath were farmed until the 14th century but subsequently abandoned to grazing, which preserved the ridge and furrow plough lines. The whole area has been colonised by a rich variety of flowers, trees and shrubs supporting many animals, birds and insects including the rare black hairstreak butterfly.

Eventually leaving the reserve, the path breaks from trees to run between arable fields. Beyond a crossing track, the way begins to lose height, opening a view to Castor church and across the Nene Valley. Reaching an embankment above the dual carriageway drop left and again cross with care.

In the field opposite, take the bridleway signed ahead, which leads to the corner of a lane at the top of Ailsworth. Follow it forward past houses to the end and go right to a second junction with Peterborough Road **H**. Turn left and, keeping with it, walk through the village back to Castor. ●

St Kyneburgha's Church

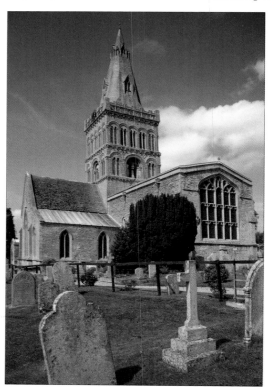

Gog Magog Hills and the Granta Valley

		GPS waypoints	
Start	Wandlebury Country Park	🖉	TL 492 532
Distance	7 miles (11.3km)	Ⓐ	TL 485 530
Approximate time	3½ hours	Ⓑ	TL 471 520
Parking	Wandlebury Country Park car park	Ⓒ	TL 475 516
Refreshments	Pubs at Stapleford	Ⓓ	TL 495 514
Ordnance Survey maps	Landranger 154 (Cambridge & Newmarket), Explorer 209 (Cambridge)	Ⓔ	TL 502 520
		Ⓕ	TL 505 536

Cambridgeshire is not renowned for its hills, but the few places where the ground does significantly rise have always drawn people. The Gog Magog Hills are no exception and betray forgotten settlement in the mounds of pre-historic burials, defensive earthworks and a Roman road. This walk to the nearby village of Stapleford, with its ancient church and pubs, wanders on along the shallow Granta Valley before returning along a pleasant stretch of the undulating Roman highway.

Occupying a commanding position and the site of earlier Stone and Bronze Age settlements, Wandlebury Ring is a fine Iron Age hillfort, defended by a deep encircling ditch and embankment over ½ mile (800m) in circumference. Thrown up in the 3rd century BC, it was reinforced during the 1st century BC and there is evidence of later Roman occupation within the enclosed area. The Anglo Saxons used the spot as a meeting place and gave it the name by which we know it today, Wendlesbiri. James II established a stud here and, in the 1730s, the second Earl Godolphin destroyed much of the ancient ramparts in extending the stables and building a house. He was owner of the famous racehorse *Godolphin Arab*, from which many of today's thoroughbreds are descended. The horse died in 1753 and

was buried beneath the cupola in the stables, the only part of the buildings to remain after the house was demolished in the 1950s.

🖉 Head back to the dual carriageway and carefully cross to a gated footpath opposite signed to Stapleford. Go right, as far as an opening on the left some 50 yds (46m) along. Turn through the right-hand one of the two gates onto Magog Down. Strike diagonally across the slope of the hill on a trod, passing a waypost to reach the far bottom corner. A contained path continues through the small plantation of Colin's Wood to emerge through gates onto Haverhill Road Ⓐ. Go left towards Stapleford.

After ¾ mile (1.2km), at the edge of the village, turn right into Gog Magog Way. Follow it to a junction by an

On the Roman road

the track later narrows to a path, eventually reaching a stile in the right-hand fence. Cut the corner of the adjacent field to a bridge and cross the River Granta **D**. Follow a track on for 200 yds (183m) before leaving through a kissing-gate on the left. Take a grass path through a young plantation, going left at a junction in the middle. Recross the river and keep ahead along the left-hand field edge. Later doglegging right and left, resume your heading to emerge onto the main road **E**.

Follow the verge right for 200 yds (183m) before crossing to a bridleway, Mile Road. It steadily rises in a dead-

island green, there going left into Bar Lane. Just before Stapleford Primary School, leave along a tarmac path on the right, Vicarage Lane, which leads through to Church Lane **B**. Built of flint, St Andrew's lies not far to the right. Amongst its interesting features, the church has an early Norman chancel arch, the sides pierced by squints to allow those seated in the aisles a view to the altar. A Saxon grave marker and Norman grave cover are also relics of its early history.

The onward route, however, continues along Church Lane in the other direction, shortly passing a small thatched flint building, a 19th-century slaughter-house, before reaching the main road by The Longbow. Turn left, passing a second pub, The Rose, before going left again into Bury Road. Where it later bends **C**, keep ahead along a track signed to Babraham and Sawston that leads past Bury Farm.

The way courses between open fields for over a mile (1.6km), giving a fine view to the Magog Hills. Keep going as

straight line towards the high ground, eventually levelling beside the tree-clad Copley Hill, which is the site of a large Bronze Age burial mound. Turning left at a junction, you are now on Via Devana, an 18th-century name for the Roman road built around AD43 between Colchester and Godmanchester. It falls pleasantly between trees and high hedges, after ¹/₂ mile (800m) reaching two adjacent paths leaving on the left **F**.

Take the second of the two, signed to Wandlebury Ring and Cambridge,

passing along a strip of woodland to a junction in front of a cottage. Go right and then keep left, the path passing new plantation and eventually meeting a junction at the edge of open space. Bear right on the obvious track that hugs the tree fringe, before rising to a tarmac track beside a bridge spanning the surrounding ditch of the ancient hillfort. Turn left back to the car park. ●

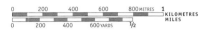

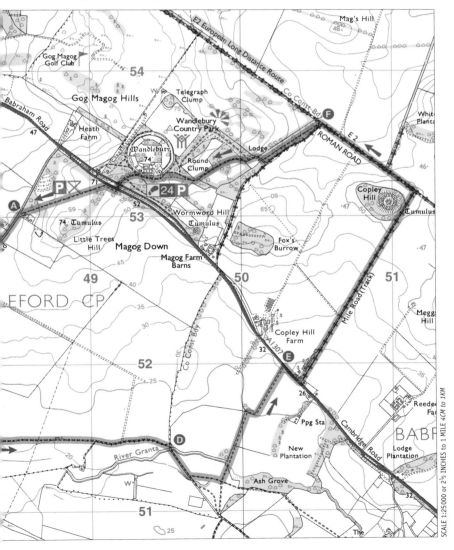

SCALE 1:25000 or 2½ INCHES to 1 MILE 4CM to 1KM

Barnack, Helpston and Ufford

		GPS waypoints
Start	Barnack, by the church	TF 078 050
Distance	7½ miles (12.1km)	Ⓐ TF 083 054
Approximate time	4 hours	Ⓑ TF 102 056
Parking	Roadside parking at Barnack	Ⓒ TF 121 054
Refreshments	Pubs at Barnack, Helpston and Ufford	Ⓓ TF 121 052
		Ⓔ TF 103 050
Ordnance Survey maps	Landranger 142 (Peterborough), Explorers 234 (Rutland Water) and 235 (Wisbech & Peterborough North)	Ⓕ TF 093 041

At Barnack, the low-lying levels give way to gently rolling hills of limestone, a warm mellow rock that has lent its character to the villages dotting the landscape. However, today's neatly hedged fields and woodland copses, through which the walk meanders, are quite different from the ragged, open heathland remembered by the Helpston poet, John Clare, during the early 19th century.

The splendid building qualities of Barnack's stone were recognised by the Romans and the quarries they began were worked throughout the medieval period. The quarries provided fine ashlar for many churches and cathedrals in the area, its widespread use enabled by the maze of channels and rivers through the fens, along which the cut stone could be transported great distances. Barnack's own church is an impressive example and illustrates the changing architectural styles of the passing centuries. The oldest part, the tower, was raised at the beginning of the 11th century in typically bold Saxon style, the long and short stonework still striking.

Almshouses in Helpston

With the church on your left, follow Main Street through a couple of bends to a T-junction with the B1443. Turn right and walk out of the village. Just after the speed de-restriction sign, a footpath marked the Torpel Way is signed off right Ⓐ. It hugs the field perimeter adjacent to the road and reaching the corner, swings away within the field. After 100

Barnack church

yds (91m) go left at a waymark along the edge of the adjoining field. Again turn with the corner, then look for a plank bridge spanning the left-hand ditch. Pass through a small wood and continue in the next field. At the far end, accompany the hedge right to the next corner, where a 'Torpel Way' sign to Ashton directs you through a gap on the left. Walk on, finally crossing a footbridge onto a lane. Over a stile breaking the opposite hedge, keep ahead across successive fields. Emerging onto a second lane on the outskirts of Ashton, follow it right to a junction in the village **B**.

Go left, but then immediately leave through a kissing-gate on the right along an enclosed path, again marked 'Torpel Way'. Wind on, eventually entering a crop field. Walk ahead at its edge and then, over a stile, bear right across a couple of paddocks, where grassy mounds and ditches outline a ring and bailey. Pass out at the far side to a junction and follow the main lane ahead to a crossroads in the centre of Helpston **C**.

Born here in 1793, John Clare is celebrated as the 'Peasant Poet'. Put to work tending sheep as a child, throughout his life he developed an intimate understanding and love of the countryside at a time when the rough heath and natural woodland were being tamed by enclosure. Clare's legacy is a

SCALE 1:25000 or 2½ INCHES to 1 MILE 4CM to 1KM

0 200 400 600 800 METRES 1
0 200 400 600 YARDS ½

KILOMETRES
MILES

unique glimpse into that world, not through the eyes of a Romantic, but one whose every day was governed by nature. He is buried in St Botolph's churchyard and remembered in an elaborate memorial of white stone, which stands at the crossroads opposite the village's 14th-century cross.

Go right along Woodgate, passing the cottage in which Clare was born. At the next junction, turn off into Broad Wheel Road ⓓ. Where it later bends by the last of the houses, bear off left onto a bridleway across the fields. Later doglegging left and right, continue at the edge of Rice Wood to a junction with the Torpel Way. Turn right and walk out to a lane. A short distance to the right leave through a waymarked gate on the left. After passing the edge of Hilly Wood, the track carries on between open fields to meet another lane ⓔ.

Follow it left for about ¼ mile (400m) to a waymarked bridge on the right.

Walk away, initially beside a wood and then a hedge. Later slipping through, continue on its opposite flank to emerge at the edge of Ufford. To the left the lane climbs into the village, reaching a junction opposite The White Hart **F**. Ufford's church, St Andrew's, stands impressively on top of the hill, and before the Reformation, was a resting place for pilgrims journeying to the Holy shrine at Walsingham.

However, the onward route lies to the right along Walcot Road. At a bend beyond the village, turn off along a short walled track on the right. Approaching the end, go left over a stile beside a house and head away at the field edge. Walk on in the next field, doglegging around its convoluted perimeter to a footbridge in the far-right bottom corner. Emerging onto a field track, a former railway trackbed, follow it right for a little over $\frac{1}{4}$ mile (400m). At a waymark, go left and, after winding through a clump of trees, swing left at the edge of the next field. Leave at the corner, where a three-way sign directs you right back to Barnack. ●

Ferry Meadows, River Nene and Peterborough

Ferry Meadows, River Nene and Peterborough

		GPS waypoints
Start	Ferry Meadows Country Park Visitor Centre	🖉 TL 148 974
Distance	10¼ miles (16.5km) - 5½ miles (8.9km) for short walk	Ⓐ TL 154 977
		Ⓑ TL 165 972
Approximate time	5¼ hours - 2¾ hours for short walk	Ⓒ TL 191 981
		Ⓓ TL 192 986
Parking	Car park by Visitor Centre	Ⓔ TL 187 982
Refreshments	Café at Visitor Centre, pubs and cafés in Peterborough	
Ordnance Survey maps	Landranger 142 (Peterborough), Explorer 227 (Peterborough)	

Contained within a sweeping bend of the River Nene, Ferry Meadows Country Park attracts both watersports enthusiasts and nature lovers. This walk explores the park and can be extended along the river into Peterborough to visit the ancient cathedral church and its precincts.

Prior to gravel extraction during the 1970s, the low-lying fields were worked as farmland and osier beds. The abandoned pits subsequently flooded to form a series of lakes, which, together with the surrounding woods and grass

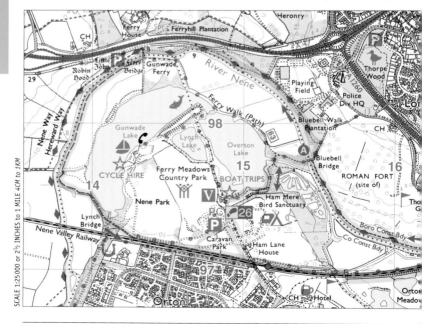

wetlands have attracted a wide range of animal and plant life. The area provides good cover for smaller birds and almost 200 species have been reported.

 Leave the car park beside the Information Centre to a broad track, where the main visitor complex lies to the left. However, keep ahead, picking up a path to Bluebell Wood, which skirts Overton Lake, the water on your left. Over a bridge, turn right, soon crossing a suspension bridge spanning the Nene Ⓐ.

A short distance beyond, leave the tarmac for a dirt path, delving into Bluebell Wood on the left, signed 'Riverside Walk'. Keep to the lower trail through the trees, later passing restored osier beds worked from the 19th century. Reaching Ferry Bridge, built in 1716 to replace the original ferry, cross and immediately turn through a gate on the right, walking away at the meadow's edge beside the river.

At the far end beyond a drain, the track briefly rejoins the river before turning away towards Gunwade Lake. Curving right, the bridleway parallels a cycle track beside the water, to a bridge

across the Nene Valley Railway. Instead of crossing, continue on a gravel path alongside the railway – part of the line from Northampton to Peterborough, it operated from 1845 until closure in 1972. The section between Wandsford Station and Peterborough was reopened to steam in 1977, worked by both British and continental engines as well as a fully operational mail coach.

Remaining on the path nearest the railway, carry on, later crossing a road. Eventually, walk over a level crossing by the entrance to Peterborough Yacht Club, and immediately go left towards Orton Mere. Approaching a car park, keep left and then turn left, crossing the railway and a bridge over Orton Lock Ⓑ.

The quick return heads back upstream to Bluebell Bridge Ⓐ, otherwise carry on to Peterborough following the tarmac cycle path right. As it then swings left, abandon it to pass beneath the road bridge. Staying close to the river,

Peterborough Cathedral

continue on a path beside Thorpe Meadows and later over a bridge, through a local nature reserve. After a second bridge, the path eventually rejoins the cycleway. Carry on beneath successive bridges and then below waterside flats. Reaching a footbridge ⓒ, turn off the promenade up steps and walk through to a shopping precinct. Almost immediately, at a signpost for the Tourist Information Centre, leave along an alley on the right and keep ahead across a service area to Bridge Street. Turn left, cross over the main road and continue up to Cathedral Square. The cathedral precincts are then reached through a medieval gateway on the right ⓓ.

Dedicated to the saints Peter, Paul and Andrew, the cathedral stands on a monastic site originally founded by King Paeda in 655. After destruction by Danish raiders in 870, it was rebuilt as a Benedictine abbey, the present church was begun in 1118 following a fire. A truly beautiful building with an exquisitely painted roof, it became a cathedral after the Dissolution in 1541; the last abbot being created its first bishop. Buried here is Catherine of Aragon, Henry VIII's first wife. For a short time after her execution, Mary Queen of Scots lay here too, her body was later reinterred within Westminster Abbey by her son, James I.

Returning to the river, go back along the embankment. However, shortly after passing beneath the last of the bridges leaving the city, bear off with the cycleway ⓔ picking up signs to Thorpe Meadows. Beyond a small housing development, swing right over a bridge and then go left towards Orton and Ferry Meadows. After passing the Boathouse pub, leave the cycleway and keep ahead by the left-hand bank of the Rowing Club's lake. Briefly rejoin your outward track beyond its end to pass beneath the road bridge to Orton Lock ⓑ. Now remaining on this bank, carry on upstream, eventually reaching Bluebell Bridge ⓐ. Cross and retrace your way back to the Visitor Centre and car park. ●

Ely and Little Downham

		GPS waypoints
Start	Ely, Tourist Information Centre	🥾 TL 537 802
Distance	10½ miles (16.9km)	Ⓐ TL 524 809
Approximate time	5½ hours	Ⓑ TL 523 838
Parking	Ely	Ⓒ TL 531 834
Refreshments	Pubs and cafés at Ely, pubs at Little Downham	Ⓓ TL 547 833
		Ⓔ TL 550 834
Ordnance Survey maps	Landranger 143 (Ely & Wisbech), Explorer 228 (March & Ely)	Ⓕ TL 566 829
		Ⓖ TL 551 808
		Ⓗ TL 556 805
		Ⓙ TL 544 798

It was the small islands of higher ground that attracted settlement within the vast marshes of the Fens, Ely and neighbouring Little Downham being just two examples. This walk between them rambles along old drove roads, where hedges and small copses provide cover for small birds in this open landscape, before finally returning to the town beside the River Great Ouse.

Little Downham has been associated with Ely for over 1,000 years, granted to the monks in 970. During the Middle Ages, the bishops established a summer palace there amidst a 250-acre (101-hectare) deer park, the sparse ruins of which can still be seen just north west of the village.

🥾 Leave the Tourist Information Centre along the main road past St Mary's Church, crossing to go left into Downham Road. Very soon, bear left again into West Fen Road and follow it out to the main A10 road. Carefully cross and carry on with the lane opposite, signed to Coveney. After ¼ mile (400m), just past a fenced compound, a byway (Green Lane) leaves on the right Ⓐ.

Beyond a barn it continues as a hedged grass track. Reaching a junction, go left on another track, Hurst Lane, bearing right where it shortly forks. The track runs between the fields towards Little Downham, its dwellings clustered on a low hill. Reaching a house after

some 1¼ miles (2km), the onward track becomes metalled and rises to the edge of the village. At a crossroads, keep ahead up Chapel Lane to Main Street at the top Ⓑ.

Turn right, passing The Anchor to reach St Leonard's Church. In the porch, there is a beautifully carved frieze of human and animal heads surmounting the Norman doorway and, inside, the coat of arms of King George III are believed to be the largest such blazon displayed in any English church. At the village green, keep ahead towards Ely, later going by the brick tower of a windmill, set back from the road. After another ¼ mile (400m), turn left into Marshal Lane Ⓒ, which quickly degrades to a track. Reaching a way-marked junction, go right and, eventually at the end turn left. Keep with the main track to meet a busy road.

Carefully cross to a track opposite, which leads to Chettisham Ⓓ. Turn beside its 13th-century church and walk

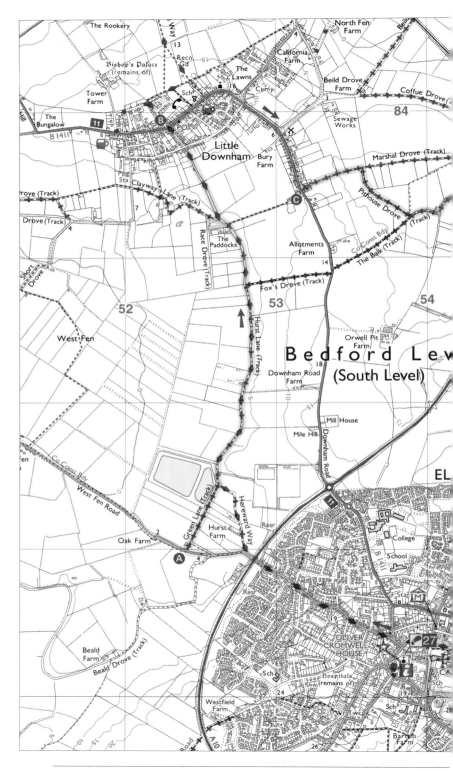

out to the main lane. Go left to a level crossing, immediately over which, leave through a gate on the right onto Kettlesworth Drove **E**. First on one side and much later the other, follow a meandering ditch across the open,

dead-flat fields for a mile (1.6km). Approaching a second railway line, turn off right by abandoned brick buildings onto a grassy track, Clayway Drove **F**.

Watch out for trains as you recross the first railway and carry on to join Prickwillow Road. Follow it ahead for ¹/₂ mile (800m), rounding a bend to

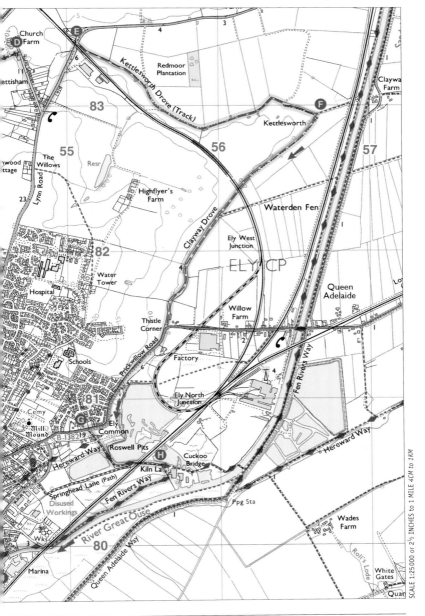

reach a waymarked metalled track on the left **G**. Walk past the Environment Agency building and between the pools of Roswell Pits Nature Reserve. Beyond another level crossing and just before a light industrial building, bear right on a tarmac path beside its car park **H**. Turn through a gate at its end, and follow a path at the edge of a meadow, soon joining the River Great Ouse. Remain with the riverside path beneath a railway bridge and then past Lincoln Bridge, to reach the Maltings. Just beyond **J**, turn away through Jubilee Park.

Crossing a road at the far side, continue into Cherry Hill Park opposite, from which there is a splendid view across to the cathedral and its majestic crown-like central lantern. Keep ahead through the medieval gateway of the Ely Porta and turn right past the old monastic buildings that became the King's School. Reaching the great west front of the cathedral, swing left across a green to return to St Mary's Church and the Tourist Information Centre. ●

Ely Cathedral from Cherry Hill Park

Grafham Water

		GPS waypoints
Start	Grafham Water Visitor Centre, off B661, 1 mile (1.6km) west of Buckden	✎ TL 166 680
Distance	9¼ miles (14.9km)	Ⓐ TL 158 686
Approximate time	5 hours	Ⓑ TL 160 697
Parking	Grafham Water Visitor Centre car park	Ⓒ TL 146 696
Refreshments	Pub at Perry, cafés at Visitor Centre and Fishing Lodge	Ⓓ TL 144 670
		Ⓔ TL 154 667
		Ⓕ TL 168 664
Ordnance Survey maps	Landranger 153 (Bedford & Huntingdon), Explorer 225 (Huntingdon & St Ives)	

Built in the 1960s and extending over 1,500 acres, Grafham Water is one of the largest lakes in the region. This walk around its perimeter at times follows a cycle trail, so keep a look out for cyclists, but in the woodland areas, several nature trails offer optional quiet detours through the trees.

The reservoir, the focus of a whole range of outdoor activities, is equally important in offering diverse wildlife habitats and much of the shore has been designated SSSI. The water attracts both migratory and resident wildfowl and there are several hides from which to observe them. Parts of the woodland are centuries old, with coppice management encouraging small birds, mammals and insects, while the open meadows are rich in grassland flowers, particularly in spring and early summer.

✎ Walk from the Visitor Centre towards the lake and follow the shore right. A developing grass path takes the way below a wood and then around a promontory before leaving the water's edge to a junction of paths Ⓐ. Through a gate, climb Church Hill into Grafham. All Saints' Church is a short detour to the left. Its rubble construction betrays the scarcity of local stone, but it is still a building of character. Light floods in through high dormer windows and corbelled roof supports are decorated with heads. There is more early carving in the porch, part of a tomb cover depicting a priest.

Go back along Church Road and turn left into Breach Road, continuing beyond the last of the houses for a further ¼ mile (400m). Signed left Ⓑ, a bridleway follows the field edge

Grafham Water near Visitor Centre

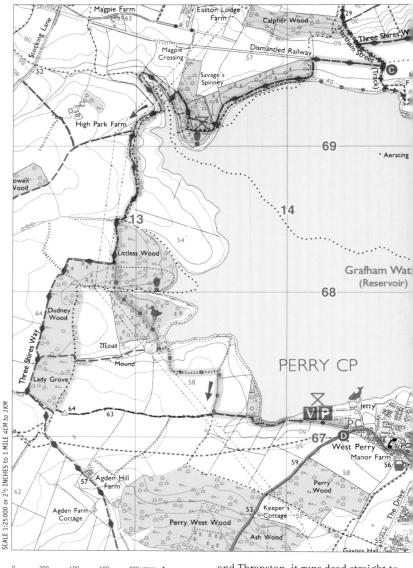

SCALE 1:25000 or 2½ INCHES to 1 MILE 4CM to 1KM

towards West Wood. Just before a gate, leave through a broad gap breaking the left-hand hedge and walk on beside the wood. Keep going in the next large field, to meet a track beyond its corner. Turn left along the boundary to a fingerpost **C**.

Bear right into the field corner, there joining a hedged grass track. Part of a former railway between Huntingdon and Thrapston, it runs dead straight to the right for ¼ mile (400m) before being blocked by bushes. Go left and right into the corner of the neighbouring field but as you pass out, look for a waymarked path immediately on the left. Dropping just inside the trees, it breaks out across a strip of flower meadow to the cycle path.

To the right, the track leads through the nature reserve, initially close to the water's edge but after a while turning up into the wood. Later emerging, it

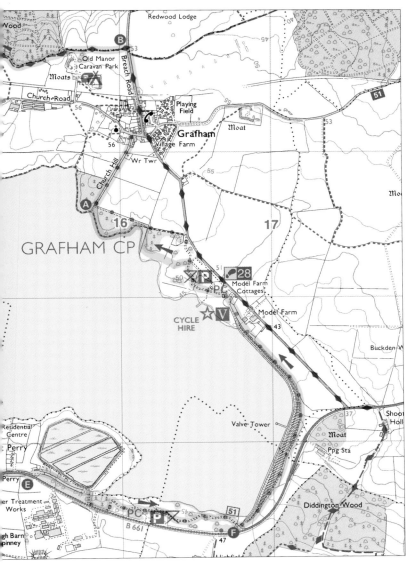

winds around a small inlet to cross a stream. Rising once more, the way undulates on beside open farmland, later bearing left to enter Littless Wood. This is the most ancient woodland within the reserve and several nature trails wander off the main path. Leaving the trees behind, the track once more climbs across open farmland, the relative height allowing a fine view across the reservoir. Dropping alongside another area of reserve, the way shortly leads past the Fishing Lodge car park to the road outside Perry **D**.

Turn left through the village, the cycle track resuming again at the far end, just before the speed de-restriction sign **E**. Winding off into trees, it meanders between the lake and road, before long passing behind another parking area. Keep going to the southern end of the dam **F**, where the path drops below the embankment. After a final climb to the service road at the far end cut behind the café back to the car park.

Further Information

 The National Trust

Anyone who likes visiting places of natural beauty and/or historic interest has cause to be grateful to the National Trust. Without it, many such places would probably have vanished by now.

It was in response to the pressures on the countryside posed by the relentless march of Victorian industrialisation that the trust was set up in 1895. Its founders, inspired by the common goals of protecting and conserving Britain's national heritage and widening public access to it, were Sir Robert Hunter, Octavia Hill and Canon Rawnsley: respectively a solicitor, a social reformer and a clergyman. The latter was particularly influential. As a canon of Carlisle Cathedral and vicar of Crosthwaite (near Keswick), he was concerned about threats to the Lake District and had already been active in protecting footpaths and promoting public access to open countryside. After the flooding of Thirlmere in 1879 to create a large reservoir, he became increasingly convinced that the only effective way to guarantee protection was outright ownership of land.

The purpose of the National Trust is to preserve areas of natural beauty and sites of historic interest by acquisition, holding them in trust for the nation and making them available for public access and enjoyment. Some of its properties have been acquired through purchase, but many have been donated. Nowadays it is not only one of the biggest landowners in the country, but also one of the most active conservation charities, protecting 581,113 acres (253,176 ha) of land, including 555 miles (892km) of coastline, and more than 300 historic properties in England, Wales and Northern Ireland. (There is a separate National Trust for Scotland, which was set up in 1931.)

Furthermore, once a piece of land has come under National Trust ownership, it is difficult for its status to be altered. As a result of parliamentary legislation in 1907, the Trust was given the right to declare its property inalienable, so ensuring that in any subsequent dispute it can appeal directly to parliament.

As it works towards its dual aims of conserving areas of attractive countryside and encouraging greater public access (not easy to reconcile in this age of mass tourism), the Trust provides an excellent service for walkers by creating new concessionary paths and waymarked trails, maintaining stiles and footbridges and combating the ever-increasing problem of footpath erosion.

For details of membership, contact the National Trust at the address on page 95.

 The Ramblers' Association

No organisation works more actively to protect and extend the rights and interests of walkers in the countryside than the Ramblers' Association. Its aims are clear: to foster a greater knowledge, love and care of the countryside; to assist in the protection and enhancement of public rights of way and areas of natural beauty; to work for greater public access to the countryside; and to encourage more people to take up rambling as a healthy, recreational leisure activity.

It was founded in 1935 when, following the setting up of a National Council of Ramblers' Federation in 1931, a number of federations in London, Manchester, the Midlands and elsewhere came together to create a more effective pressure group, to deal with such problems as the disappearance or obstruction of footpaths, the prevention of access to open mountain and moorland, and increasing hostility from landowners. This was the era of the mass trespasses, when there were sometimes violent confrontations between ramblers and gamekeepers, especially on the moorlands of the Peak District.

Since then the Ramblers' Association

Along Blind Lane

has played a key role in preserving and developing the national footpath network, supporting the creation of national parks and encouraging the designation and waymarking of long-distance routes.

Our freedom of access to the country-side, now enshrined in legislation, is still in its early years and requires constant vigilance. But over and above this there will always be the problem of footpaths being illegally obstructed, disappearing through lack of use, or being extinguished by housing or road construction.

It is to meet such problems and dangers that the Ramblers' Association exists and represents the interests of all walkers. The address to write to for information on the Ramblers' Association and how to become a member is given on page 95.

 ### Walkers and the Law

The *Countryside and Rights of Way Act 2000 (CRoW)* extends the rights of access previously enjoyed by walkers in England and Wales. Implementation of these rights began on 19 September 2004. The Act amends existing legislation and for the first time provides access on foot to certain types of land – defined as mountain, moor, heath, down and registered common land.

Where You Can Go
Rights of Way
Prior to the introduction of *CRoW* walkers could only legally access the countryside along public rights of way. These are either 'footpaths' (for walkers only) or 'bridleways' (for walkers, riders on horseback and pedal cyclists). A third category called 'Byways open to all traffic' (BOATs), is used by motorised vehicles as well as those using non-mechanised transport. Mainly they are green lanes, farm and estate roads, although occasionally they will be found crossing mountainous area.

Rights of way are marked on Ordnance Survey maps. Look for the green broken lines on the Explorer maps, or the red dashed lines on Landranger maps.

The term 'right of way' means exactly what it says. It gives a right of passage over what, for the most part, is private land. Under pre-CRoW legislation walkers were required to keep to the line of the right of way and not stray onto land on either side. If you did inadvertently wander off the right of way, either because of faulty map reading or because the route was not clearly indicated on the ground, you were technically trespassing.

Local authorities have a legal obligation to ensure that rights of way are kept clear and free of obstruction, and are signposted where they leave metalled roads. The duty of local authorities to install signposts extends to the placing of signs along a path or way, but only where the authority considers it necessary to have a signpost or waymark to assist persons unfamiliar with the locality.

The New Access Rights
Access Land
As well as being able to walk on existing rights of way, under the new legislation you now have access to large areas of open land. You can of course continue to use rights of way footpaths to cross this land, but the main difference is that you can now law-fully leave the path and wander at will, but only in areas designated as access land.

Further Information

Countryside Access Charter

Your rights of way are:

- public footpaths – on foot only. Sometimes waymarked in yellow
- bridleways – on foot, horseback and pedal cycle. Sometimes waymarked in blue
- byways (usually old roads), most 'roads used as public paths' and, of course, public roads – all traffic has the right of way

Use maps, signs and waymarks to check rights of way. Ordnance Survey Explorer and Landranger maps show most public rights of way

On rights of way you can:

- take a pram, pushchair or wheelchair if practicable
- take a dog (on a lead or under close control)
- take a short route round an illegal obstruction or remove it sufficiently to get past

You have a right to go for recreation to:

- public parks and open spaces – on foot
- most commons near older towns and cities – on foot and sometimes on horseback
- private land where the owner has a formal agreement with the local authority

In addition you can use the following by local or established custom or consent, but ask for advice if you are unsure:

- many areas of open country, such as moorland, fell and coastal areas, especially those in the care of the National Trust, and some commons
- some woods and forests, especially those owned by the Forestry Commission
- country parks and picnic sites
- most beaches
- canal towpaths
- some private paths and tracks Consent sometimes extends to horse-riding and cycling

For your information:

- county councils and London boroughs maintain and record rights of way, and register commons
- obstructions, dangerous animals, harassment and misleading signs on rights of way are illegal and you should report them to the county council
- paths across fields can be ploughed, but must normally be reinstated within two weeks
- landowners can require you to leave land to which you have no right of access
- motor vehicles are normally permitted only on roads, byways and some 'roads used as public paths'

Where to Walk

Areas now covered by the new access rights – Access Land – are shown on Ordnance Survey Explorer maps bearing the access land symbol on the front cover.

'Access Land' is shown on Ordnance Survey maps by a light yellow tint surrounded by a pale orange border. New orange coloured 'i' symbols on the maps will show the location of permanent access information boards installed by the access authorities.

Restrictions

The right to walk on access land may lawfully be restricted by landowners.

Landowners can, for any reason, restrict access for up to 28 days in any year. They cannot however close the land:

- on bank holidays;
- for more than four Saturdays and Sundays in a year;
- on any Saturday from 1 June to 11 August; or
- on any Sunday from 1 June to the end of September.

They have to provide local authorities with five working days' notice before the date of closure unless the land involved is an area of less than five hectares or the closure is for less than four hours. In these cases landowners only need to provide two hours' notice.

Whatever restrictions are put into place

on access land they have no effect on existing rights of way, and you can continue to walk on them.

Dogs

Dogs can be taken on access land, but must be kept on leads of two metres or less between 1 March and 31 July, and at all times where they are near livestock. In addition landowners may impose a ban on all dogs from fields where lambing takes place for up to six weeks in any year. Dogs may be banned from moorland used for grouse shooting and breeding for up to five years.

In the main, walkers following the routes in this book will continue to follow existing rights of way, but a knowledge and understanding of the law as it affects walkers, plus the ability to distinguish access land marked on the maps, will enable anyone who wishes to depart from paths that cross access land either to take a shortcut, to enjoy a view or to explore.

General Obstructions

Obstructions can sometimes cause a problem on a walk and the most common of these is where the path across a field has been ploughed over. It is legal for a farmer to plough up a path provided that it is restored within two weeks. This does not always happen and you are faced with the dilemma of following the line of the path, even if this means treading on crops, or walking round the edge of the field. Although the later course of action seems the most sensible, it does mean that you would be trespassing.

Other obstructions can vary from overhanging vegetation to wire fences across the path, locked gates or even a cattle feeder on the path.

Use common sense. If you can get round the obstruction without causing damage, do so. Otherwise only remove as much of the obstruction as is necessary to secure passage.

If the right of way is blocked and cannot be followed, there is a long-standing view that in such circumstances there is a right to deviate, but this cannot

Pretty cottage in Helpston

wholly be relied on. Although it is accepted in law that highways (and that includes rights of way) are for the public service, and if the usual track is impassable, it is for the general good that people should be entitled to pass into another line. However, this should not be taken as indicating a right to deviate whenever a way becomes impassable. If in doubt, retreat.

Report obstructions to the local authority and/or the Ramblers' Association.

 ## Global Positioning System (GPS)

What is GPS?

GPS is a worldwide radio navigation system that uses a network of 24 satellites and receivers, usually hand-held, to calculate positions. By measuring the time it takes a signal to reach the receiver, the distance from the satellite can be estimated. Repeat this with several satellites and the receiver can then use triangulation to establish the position of the receiver.

How to use GPS with Ordnance Survey mapping

Each of the walks in this book includes GPS co-ordinate data that reflects the walk position points on Ordnance Survey maps.

GPS and OS maps use different models for the earth and co-ordinate systems, so when you are trying to relate your GPS position to features on the map the two will differ slightly. This is especially the case with height, as the model that relates the GPS global co-ordinate system to height above sea level is very poor.

When using GPS with OS mapping, some distortion – up to 16ft (5m) – will always be present. Moreover, individual features on maps may have been surveyed only to an accuracy of 23ft (7m) (for 1:25000 scale maps), while other features, e.g. boulders, are usually only shown schematically.

In practice, this should not cause undue difficulty, as you will be near enough to your objective to be able to spot it.

How to use the GPS data in this book
There are various ways you can use the GPS data in this book.

1. Follow the route description while checking your position on your receiver when you are approaching a position point.

2. You can also use the positioning information on your receiver to verify where you are on the map.

3. Alternatively, you can use some of the proprietary software that is available. At the simple end there is inexpensive software, which lets you input the walk positions (waypoints), download them to the gps unit and then use them to assist your navigation on the walks.

At the upper end of the market Ordnance Survey maps are available in electronic form. Most come with software that enables you to enter your walking route onto the map, download it to your gps unit and use it, alongside the route description, to follow the route.

Walking Safety

Although the reasonably gentle countryside that is the subject of this book offers no real dangers to walkers at any time of the year, it is still advisable to take sensible precautions and follow certain well-tried guidelines.

Always take with you both warm and waterproof clothing and sufficient food

and drink. Wear suitable footwear such as strong walking boots or shoes that give a good grip over stony ground, on slippery slopes and in muddy conditions. Try to obtain a local weather forecast and bear it in mind before you start. Do not be afraid to abandon your proposed route and return to your starting point in the event of a sudden and unexpected deterioration in the weather.

All the walks described in this book will be safe to do, given due care and respect, even during the winter. Indeed, a crisp, fine winter day often provides perfect walking conditions, with firm ground underfoot and a clarity unique to this time of the year. The most difficult hazard likely to be encountered is mud, especially when walking along woodland and field paths, farm tracks and bridleways – the latter in particular can often get churned up by cyclists and horses. In summer, an additional difficulty may be narrow and overgrown paths, particularly along the edges of cultivated fields. Neither should constitute a major problem provided that the appropriate footwear is worn.

Useful Organisations

Cambridgeshire County Council
Environment Division,
Shire Hall, Castle Hill,
Cambridge CB3 0AP
Tel. 01223 717445
www.cambridgeshire.gov.uk

Campaign to Protect Rural England
128 Southwark Street,
London SE1 0SW
Tel. 020 7981 2800
www.cpre.org.uk

Camping and Caravanning Club
Greenfields House, Westwood Way,
Coventry CV4 8JH
Site bookings tel. 0845 130 7633
www.campingandcaravanningclub.co.uk

Forestry Commission
Silvan House, 231 Corstorphine Road,
Edinburgh EH12 7AT

Tel. 0131 334 0303
www.forestry.gov.uk

Long Distance Walkers' Association
www.ldwa.org.uk

National Trust
Membership and general enquiries:
PO Box 39, Warrington
WA5 7WD
Tel. 0870 458 4000
www.nationaltrust.org.uk
East Anglia Regional Office:
Westley Bottom, Bury St Edmunds,
Suffolk IP33 3WD
Tel. 01284 747500

Natural England
1 East Parade, Sheffield S1 2ET
Tel. 0114 241 8920
www.naturalengland.org.uk

Ordnance Survey
Romsey Road, Maybush,
Southampton SO16 4GU
Tel. 08456 05 05 05 (Lo-call)
www.ordnancesurvey.co.uk

Ramblers' Association
2nd Floor, Camelford House,
87–90 Albert Embankment,
London SE1 7TW
Tel. 020 7339 8500
www.ramblers.org.uk

Tourist information:
East of England Tourism
Dettingen House, Dettingen Way,
Bury St. Edmunds,
Suffolk IP33 3TU
Tel. 01284 727470
www.visiteastofengland.com

Local tourist information centres:
Cambridge: 0871 226 8006
Ely: 01353 662062
Peterborough: 01733 452336
St Neots: 01480 388788
Wisbech: 01945 583263

Peterborough City Council
Bayard Place, Broadway,

Peterborough PE1 1FB
Tel. 01733 747474
www.peterborough.gov.uk

Youth Hostels Association
Trevelyan House,
Dimple Road, Matlock,
Derbyshire DE4 3YH
Tel. 01629 592600
www.yha.org.uk

 Ordnance Survey maps of Cambridgeshire and the Fens
The area of Cambridgeshire is covered by
Ordnance Survey 1:50 000 (1¼ inches to
1 mile or 2cm to 1km) scale Landranger
map sheets 142, 143, 153, 154. These all-
purpose maps are packed with information
to help you explore the area. Viewpoints,
picnic sites, places of interest and caravan
and camping sites are shown, as well as
public rights of way information such as
footpaths and bridleways.

To examine the area in more detail and
especially if you are planning walks,
Explorer maps at 1:25 000 (2½ inches to
1 mile or 4cm to 1km) scale are ideal:

208 Bedford & St Neots
209 Cambridge
210 Newmarket & Haverhill
225 Huntingdon & St Ives
226 Ely & Newmarket
227 Peterborough
228 March & Ely
234 Rutland Water
235 Wisbech & Peterborough North
236 King's Lynn, Downham Market &
       Swaffham

To get to the Cambridgeshire area use the
Ordnance Survey OS Travel Map-Route
Great Britain at 1:625 000 (1 inch to 10
miles or 4cm to 25km) scale or Ordnance
Survey OS Travel Map-Road 5 (East
Midlands and East Anglia including
London) or 8 (South East England includ-
ing London) at 1:250 000 (1 inch to 4
miles or 1cm to 2.5km) scale. Ordnance
Survey maps and guides are available
from most booksellers, stationers and
newsagents

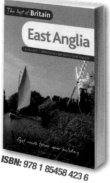

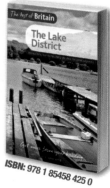